Praise for *What Great Bra...*

"What an inspired book! These are great lessons for marketing, and for life. Tracy's six principles are elegant in their simplicity, but are born from a lifetime of working with—and closely studying—great brands. This is a great book to share with everyone who touches your brand!"

— **Sidney Falken**, Chief Branding Officer, Hanes

What Great Brands Know offers precisely what's been missing from marketing for too long: a framework for integrating human, creative thinking with business strategy—an integration that's required to create inspiring brands. Great brands are built with passion and a relentless focus on providing value to the customer—not through "branding," which is often a superficial and hollow process. In this book, Carlson offers a warm, welcome and accessible path to creating compelling brands."

— **Eric Almquist**, Partner, Bain & Company

"Today's business owners need both/and thinking to successfully reach customers and stand out in the marketplace. *What Great Brands Know* will help you achieve the best of both. Drawn from compelling real-world examples, Carlson's systematic and practical framework will satisfy your orderly left-brain while providing plenty of fun and accessible right-brain boosters to ignite your creative mind and transform your work."

— **Jennifer Lee**, author of *The Right-Brain Business Plan*

"Carlson's intelligent little book decodes how truly great brands create their magic—and lights a persuasive path for you and others to follow. You may not approach marketing in quite the same way again after reading *What Great Brands Know*—and that would be good for everyone, businesses and consumers alike."

— **Bill Gentner**, President, Kao Consumer Products, Americas, Europe, Middle East & Africa

"In *What Great Brands Know*, Tracy Carlson illustrates breakthrough strategies to garner consumer's attention and loyalty, sorely needed in today's competitive and rapidly changing marketplace. With clear and engaging prose, this book provides fresh examples of successful brands as well as steps any individual or organization can employ to unleash similar creativity."

– **LeeAnne Baer**, Executive Director, Consumer Research
and Insights at Time, Inc.

"In her book, Tracy Carlson smartly explains how the art of commerce combines with emotional engagement to explain why successful brands live in the lives of their consumers. If you are looking for a place to start on how to make your brand sing, this book provides an excellent hymnal. I am giving this book to everyone in my marketing department so they can learn how to turn our brands into icons. Thank you, Tracy Carlson."

– **Marc Rovner**, General Manager, Consumer Healthcare
at Boehringer Ingelheim

"*What Great Brands Know* reveals the patterns of ingenuity that animate the products and companies we love. With left-brain lucidity and right-brain insight, Carlson illuminates what we have sensed dimly: product quality has a human quality. The good news is that product genius can be nurtured, and this finely crafted book delights its readers as it shows the way."

– **Eleanor Brown**, James Irvine Professor of Economics, Pomona College

"In this book, Tracy demonstrates how the most successful companies blend intuition with data, and sheds light on how right brain marketers can achieve breakthroughs by valuing intuition, creativity and passion. Tracy connects the dots to help us build narratives that enhance rather than oppose data."

– **Louise Dubé**, Managing Director of Digital Learning at WGBH

What Great Brands Know

Unleash Your Right-Brain Genius to
Stand Out and Make Customers Care

Tracy Carlson

Illustrations by Peter Elwell

What Great Brands Know
Unleash Your Right-Brain Genius to Stand Out and Make Customers Care
By Tracy Carlson
Longstocking Press

Published by Longstocking Press
Newton, Massachusetts, USA

Illustrations: Peter Elwell

Cover design: Annie Smidt, www.durablecreative.com

Interior design and layout: Bella Guzmán, www.HighwireCreative.com

Library of Congress Control Number: 2013917220
ISBN: 978-0-9900039-0-8

ATTENTION CORPORATIONS, UNIVERSITIES, COLLEGES AND PROFESSIONAL ORGANIZATIONS: Quantity discounts are available on bulk purchases of this book for educational, gift purposes, or as premiums for increasing magazine subscriptions or renewals. Special books or book excerpts can also be created to fit specific needs. For information, please contact orders@longstockingpress.com.

To Alex, Maggie, and Nick,
who make my life whole.

Table of Contents

66

Thus every matter, if it is to be done well,
requires the whole person.

Martin Luther

INTRODUCTION

Whether you're a leader inside an organization or run your own business, trying to grow your brand is harder than ever. Heck, it's tough enough just to hold your ground.

You know you won't get where you want to be by going the safe, incremental route. But you also know that brilliant, game-changing ideas to stand out and connect with customers tend not to drop from the sky. So what do you do?

Money's tight, but even if you had the budget, who would you hire that can really help you leapfrog? You haven't been too impressed with what you've seen. Despite the flash, the agencies and consultants all feel a little stale.

Besides, you're going flat out as it is. You've got plans to meet, numbers to make, a pipeline to fill. So you just go with something safe for the new offering or the next campaign. Path of least resistance. With barely a second to breathe, thinking expansively just doesn't make the list.

And if you're in a big company, the internal challenges can be every bit as daunting. The call for Bold New Ideas! for innovative products and approaches turns out to be only lip service (again). When push comes to shove, no one wants to take a real risk. The same old hoops for approval still dangle. You know that's just not going to move the needle, and you're getting mighty tired of the dance.

You want more

Deep down you know you should be thinking more holistically—especially about your customer. Your company, maybe your entire industry, is in a rut, looking at things too narrowly. It feels flat and lifeless. And you know if you don't find some deeper way to connect with people—well, then it's just going to be all about price. That's frustrating. (Besides, it's boring.)

Meanwhile, you can't help but envy the few brands out there that seem to be slightly magical. It's not just their success you admire—it's their creativity and how they've actually changed people's lives. But try as you might, you can't connect what they do with your own situation. Yes, it's all very well if you're Apple or Google, but what about the rest of us?

It can feel pretty disheartening. Your category is crammed with the ho-hum, with more on the horizon. Oh, for a little inspiration! To make a difference at the end of the day! Wouldn't it be nice to feel a quickening of something genuinely new and different? Glimpse the possibility of transformation?

Another way...

Stop. Take a deep breath. Relax. There are fresh, powerful ideas and approaches available. They may cost little or nothing. And, in fact, they are just inches away.

But first, consider this:

In business (and especially business school), what are we taught? To analyze. Focus on the facts. Think logically.

These are good things, and they fill our days. We can get pretty fancy with them, too. We look at the role and interplay of variables. We parse correlation vs. causality. We track, compare, segment, chart, survey, slice, and dice. Numbers rule, and we can never get enough of them. Every year, new and more powerful tools help us crunch ever-mightier reams of data.

Much of this is important and necessary.

Some of it is genius.

Some of it is extraneous and butt covering.

Some of it is downright soul killing.

It can be hard to tell the difference.

All of it, however, comes from one place: the left brain. The part of us that is deeply concerned with what we already know to be important. What we can name and measure. What we can approach logically. What seems to shine with objectivity and abstract truth.

This is what gives us some security that we are doing the right thing in a data-rich world where the stakes are very high.

This is also what gives us the safe and incremental. What crams our categories with the ho-hum. What leads to stale offerings and a zero-sum market.

In my twenty-plus years in business and marketing, I have come to realize that the world-changing stuff doesn't come from there. Instead, it comes from places that are harder to describe.

A sudden awareness.

The gentle insistence of a feeling.

The glimpsing of a shape or pattern.

An empathic understanding.

A flash of imagination.

A vision of how unrelated things connect.

These are wispy origins, especially next to the hallowed halls of Logic, Analysis, and Mathematics. Yet these are the very source of the quantum insights and discoveries we seek. And they all come from another place: the right brain.

Where the breakthroughs are

In my experience leading brands like Dove and Hellmann's and consulting to companies from the Fortune 500 to startups, it's right-brain thinking that allowed me to spot things others didn't see. A hunch led me to investigate the issue of childhood obesity—a decade before any food and beverage brands had it on their radar screen. In the commoditized world of bar soaps, inklings led me to develop new concepts using flavors as fragrances (before The Body Shop and its imitators), with off-the-charts results on a project that had bedeviled my predecessors for years.

Time and again the nonlinear approach, the emotional understanding, the perception of symbolic connection has inspired the breakthrough.

And I am not alone. While I've been bringing my right brain intuitively to my work for over twenty years, for the past few years I've focused specifically on how right-brain thinking applies to brands and business. And I've come to see that the brands we all consider special—the Targets, Southwest Airlines, Trader Joe's, and Apples of the world—are deeply imbued with right-brain genius along with classic left-brain smarts. Their counterparts (like Walmart, United, Safeway, and Microsoft) are not.

As we seek to transform our brands, to make richer connections with people, we need not look outward exclusively. Nature has provided us with a handy resource right inside, tucked next to that magnificent left hemisphere that business loves so well. We need more business folk to realize that the right brain is also a source of deep intelligence and immense value. We just need to understand it, honor it, and develop it like a muscle so we can harness our full power and potential.

In my own work, with limited or fixed budgets, I drew upon a rich reservoir of opportunities by leveraging what nature is teaching us. Nature has given two halves of a whole—and they work best when they work together.

You don't need my guidance on operational efficiency or quantitative analysis. That's not my expertise. Besides, you may have that down cold already, or if not, you can find some great resources to help you learn. But what the heck do you do with the right brain in a brand and business context? That's where I come in, and what this book is for.

This means you

You may be leading a team or company poised to make a difference. You may be a change agent within your organization, eager to find new ideas and approaches that work. You may be an emerging leader; a marketer who gets it, a product developer who knows something has to change. You may be a small business owner turned off by what the business world says you should be doing. Or you may be someone who's simply curious and interested in the business world and what it means culturally, socially, and artistically.

In the pages that follow I'll give you a framework for understanding and applying right-brain thinking to marketing and business issues. As you read, you'll get a fresh understanding of what truly iconic brands share that distinguishes them from their competitors. Differences not only in what they **do**, but how they **think**. You'll glimpse why some approaches feel right and work well, while other outwardly similar ones just fall short. You'll start to make connections with your own situation, and along the way I'll share some ideas and approaches for getting started.

And it doesn't stop there. As you identify and learn to incorporate these right-brain principles into your projects and work, you'll also notice something else: you'll feel better. More whole, more human—as nature intended.

Why am I doing this?

With a staggering quantity of books about branding out there already, why on earth does the world need another? Plenty has also been written on the right brain, starting with two excellent books to which I am deeply indebted: Daniel Pink's *A Whole New Mind*, and Iain McGilchrist's *The Master and His Emissary*. So why this?

These are ideas I am passionate about, and they have never been more necessary. This is missionary work, people.

This book is the natural outcome of 20+ years in the thick of marketing strategy for brands at organizations like Unilever, General Mills, and MIT where I often felt: *something big and important is missing here.*

This book stems in part from my own curiosity. Why do I shudder when I see companies like Microsoft, Verizon, and Bank of America on lists of best brands? (Would anyone really shed a tear if they vaporized overnight?) Why do other brands make me want to write a thank-you note or love letter? I know I'm far from alone.

There may be no shortage of brands or companies, but **there is a desperate shortage of ones we truly care about**. Ones that genuinely brighten our lives, ones we'd mourn if they disappeared tomorrow.

There are also people like you out there, eager to make a difference. You want your work to matter. You're frustrated and restless. You sense that something fundamental is missing—and you're right.

I'm writing this for you because it works. And because it feels better.

A few years ago I started Right-Brain Brands and began sending my newsletters out to the universe. I have been honored and humbled by the response. Overwhelmingly the feedback has been:

Yes!
Right on!
Way overdue.
Damn—that explains it!
Amen.

Integrating right-brain principles results in a larger, warmer, and more deeply human approach to business. This has struck a chord with lots of people, and I'm hoping it will with you, too.

The time is ripe for change

The past few decades have wrought a sea change in business and society. Newly accessible sources and overwhelming quantities of information have ushered in new grounds for decision-making—and a new cadre of masters. Left-brain expertise, in the form of analytical rigor and metrics, has properly displaced a lot of fuzzy thinking and impulsive subjectivity.

But permit me a soapbox moment: the pendulum has swung too far. We are not just bundles of data waiting to be charted, guys. We're still people, with dreams and quirks and passions. We're much more complex and interesting than you think. Only a few brands and companies really get this and meet us where we are.

Business is too important to our economy and our everyday lives to reside solely in the hands of technocrats. Just as we need both a left and right brain to thrive, so do we need whole-brain thinking—and the talents of both left- and right-brainers. We all lose when we're missing the rich and vital contribution of these different voices and approaches.

Imagine briefly a world where our enterprises hum with the combined talents of engineers, economists—and English majors. Where there is room for programming and poetry, analysis and art, spreadsheets and soul. Both/and. Places of collaboration, of free-range thinking and kick-ass execution. And honestly, doesn't that world sound like a lot more fun?

Okay, then. Let's get this started.

ABOUT THE BOOK

Now that you're eager to unleash your right-brain genius, here's a quick overview of what you'll find in the pages ahead:

How Great Brands Are Born:

Here we'll set the stage. After spending a bit more time on the left and right brains, we'll show how (singly and in combination) they give us an entirely new way to look at brands.

- You'll see why some brands are "successful" but leave us cold—while others make us cheer for them.

- You'll have a chance to apply this perspective to your own product/service and to your competitors.

What Great Brands Know and Use to Make an Impact—The Six Principles:

Here you'll find a framework that's easy to grasp and remember, using concepts beginning with the first six letters of the alphabet.*

---

*Most idea books (especially in business) offer a structural device to make them memorable. Usually it's an acronym (like SUCCESS! or SCORE!), which feels contrived and utilitarian, rarely leaving much sense of spaciousness around the ideas. A few hardy souls attempt to use the entire alphabet—but this is equally artificial (and gets pretty flimsy around Q, X and Z). The framework here arose organically. After working out the ideas needing expression and trying on different options, a six-letter approach (with three related ideas each) offered the best balance of maximum ease and minimal contrivance.

Within each principle you'll find:

- **An overview:** What this principle is about, and how it differs from what prevails in marketing and business today.

- **Three dimensions:** There are three facets to each principle. For each we'll define what it is (and isn't), and why it matters.

- **Brand Spotlights:** We'll bring each dimension to life with a brief case study. Some brands are famous, others aren't. All have earned their distinctiveness by investing their blood, sweat and tears in right-brain approaches. They haven't bought their success through heaps of advertising over time—an approach that's unavailable in today's fragmented media world, unless you have unlimited resources (and who does?).

- **Getting Started:** At the end of each principle, we'll provide ideas for getting started with that principle, most of which will be low or no cost. These suggestions will be aimed at getting more familiar with the ideas, which is an absolute prerequisite—there are no one-size-fits-all instant applications (for wouldn't that be a very left-brain approach indeed?).

The Way Forward

Here you'll find ways to make the case for integrating right-brain thinking based on three specific issues that prevail in a left-brain business world. In addition, we'll recap the Six Principles and suggest areas ripe for initial application.

Appendix: Ready for More?

Here you'll find additional resources, including a curated list of books and videos for exploring these ideas in greater depth.

HOW GREAT
BRANDS ARE BORN

66

The intuitive mind is a sacred gift and the
rational mind is a faithful servant. We have
created a society that honors the servant
and has forgotten the gift.

ALBERT EINSTEIN

Anatomy of a great brand

Before we talk about the principles that go into creating great brands, we need to take a quick peek under the hood. What do great brands really look like? How are they developed? As you'll see, they don't happen by accident. They happen precisely because their organizations choose to invest in and integrate approaches that ordinary brands don't.

To see what great brands are like and what they do differently from ordinary brands, we'll start with…

A (very brief) tale of two brains

The brain is a miraculously complex and fascinating organ. The two hemispheres, left and right, work together on most everything we do, but each has its strong suits. Here's a quick overview.

Generally speaking, the left hemisphere is the MBA of the brain, the analytical whiz kid. It's all about what's linear, sequential, logical. Focusing narrowly on what is already known to be important, it excels at context-free abstractions (and it's good at math!). It pins the known down with language and plays a starring role when manipulating what is isolated and static, creating categories and systems.[1]

By contrast, the right brain is more artist and free-range observer. It understands context, symbols, meaning, and emotional tonality. Complementing the left brain's narrow focus on the known, the right offers broad attention to the world and vigilance toward the potentially unexpected. While the left deals methodically with what is general, lifeless, constant, and discrete, the right deals with living beings and individuals, with things that are evolving and interconnected. It detects patterns and relationships and offers holistic, nonlinear, intuitive thinking.

One more thing: The left brain can make a case for itself through language. The right brain cannot. That's why I'm here: to give the right brain a voice and make a case for it.

Playing favorites

Given this division of labor, is it any wonder that business favors the left brain? As humans we have—and use—both hemispheres all the time. But business (not to mention society) explicitly reveres what the left brain does best. It's what we train for in business schools and increasingly in colleges (even elementary and secondary schools).

This preference is understandable: the world is a messy and sometimes overwhelming place. Especially now, the stakes for businesses are rising daily through relentless competition, increasing consolidation, and an explosion of data. Of course we value the left brain's ability to pinpoint, dissect, and make sense of the pieces. It creates order, giving us a sense of control in a complex world. Left-brain processes are essential and invaluable, and they often give us an edge, even if that edge is ever more fleeting.

And yet...left-brain smarts are not enough. As I'll show in this book, the brands using ample doses of right-brain thinking, too, are the standouts, the knockouts, the ones we love. Fully whole-brain brands are the ones that rock the world. Though they may not say it in so many words, they know *the right brain is where the magic is.*

A visit from an old friend

By now, right-brainers get this intuitively. You're probably nodding along or pumping your fists: Yesssss!!!!!

Left-brainers are leaning back, arms crossed, one eyebrow raised: Oh, really? So let me try to make the case in a way that works for you (or your bosses), too. I'll use the left-brainer's trusted friend, the 2 x 2 matrix.

Business students and others have been raised on matrix thinking, and the 2 x 2 is a classic way to sort, plot, express, or otherwise convey concepts with a couple of dimensions by using a chart or graph with four quadrants.

But's it's not just for the b-school set! Even Steve Jobs used it famously, not long after returning to Apple in 1996. In his absence, the product line had spun out of control. Grabbing a marker and drawing a chart with two rows and two columns, Jobs declared that henceforth Apple would offer only two types of computers, Desktop and Portable (the rows) for two audiences, Consumer and Pro (the columns). Breathtakingly simple—and effective.

The traditional path to biz success

As we think about brands (and businesses), we'll make our matrix graph-style, using axes that reflect the two dimensions of Left- and Right-Brain Development, from low to high levels of each.

First, let's look at the axis of left-brain (LB) development.

PLODDER: In the least desirable, lower-left square (low on both LB and RB development), the Plodder is a brand (or company) that pokes along. No great idea, but it dwells in a category where big ideas don't matter that much (at least yet). It may operate in an environment of relatively low competition (perhaps a local or regional brand) and/or low margins, but it knows the terrain well enough to survive, if not thrive. It's got its low-level game down and does enough to get by. For now.

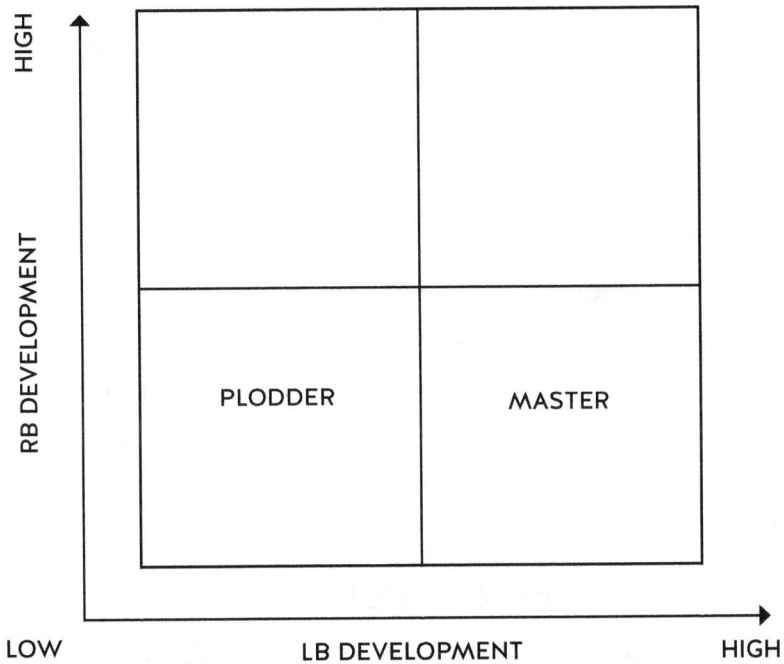

MASTER: As a brand gets better at left-brain business strategies, it may advance toward becoming a Master. It pulls ahead of its rivals by developing skills like operational efficiency and analytical horsepower that allow it to improve good stuff like margins and distribution. These growing capabilities make it a formidable competitor. It may even figure out a key strategic edge that allows it to lock in its advantages early. A retailer may secure the best locations, a software platform may become the standard in an emerging area, and so forth.

And how does the Plodder hone left-brain skills to become a Master? In ways too numerous to count. This is the classic province of business, and business school. Analytics, benchmarking, segmentation, business process reengineering, cost reduction, price optimization, outsourcing—you name it, there are infinite ways to get better at this vital left-brain stuff.

In fact, this is what we think business is all about these days. It's why businesses hire the pricey consulting firms and the engineering grads and the modelers and the outsourcing specialists. It's also why the numerate may be flocking to major in Economics instead of History or Comp Lit—not necessarily because they love it, but to be employable (and to pay back their college loans).

Wherefore art thou, right brain?

And where is the right brain in all of this? Doesn't it matter?

Absolutely! So far, though, we're talking about situations in which right-brain aspects don't matter **enough** to offset what the Master is able to offer: things like low prices, widespread distribution, convenience, and good-enough quality.

Perhaps it's a commodity category where no one cares that much. Perhaps no one has yet offered something that makes us care— or reconsider what matters most to us in this product or service area.

Perhaps the left-brain Master has eaten the lunch of its less sophisticated right-brained competitors, a frequent occurrence.

Or, quite likely, the Master may have jazzed up its offering by doing just enough on the right-brain side to grab (or rent) sales and market share. This happens a lot. The right-brain stuff is outsourced to "creative specialists" in areas like advertising and design. Whole industries spring up around the concept of "brand." These are people hired to breathe life into a desiccated little bundle of words and numbers. (Trust me—I've done this.) These right-brain specialists are called in, often at the last minute, to wave their wands and create some magic, maybe even save the brand or the company.

Meanwhile, back on the right side...

Let's get back to our matrix. ("About time!" say our left-brained friends.)

BRIGHT IDEA: In the upper left quadrant (high RB, low LB), the Bright Idea is where a lot of brands start. An entrepreneur with a passion develops a following. Or someone with a quirky idea captures the public imagination for a moment. The idea is the thing: it finds resonance with an audience willing to pay for it. For now.

The challenge here is to grow the Bright Idea into a sustainable business. The quirky idea simply may not have legs: it's a fad (Pet Rock, anyone?). It doesn't have anywhere to go. Or it may have limited appeal; if it's lucky it ends up serving a small niche. But a lot of Bright Ideas do have potential to grow—if the business can do what it needs to do: expand its distribution and customer base, improve its margin, fend off competitors, etc.

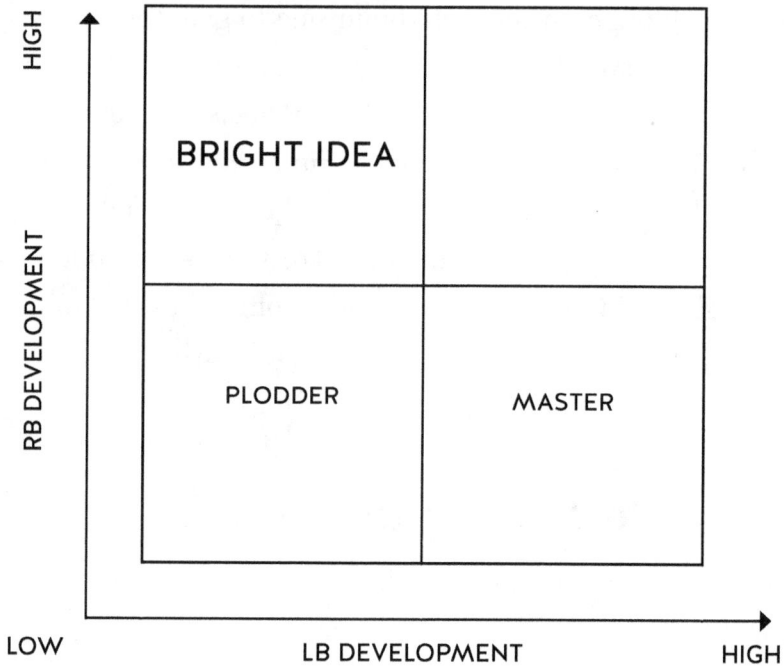

Much of what the Bright Idea needs is traditional left-brain business skills: financial acumen, efficient operations, smart sourcing strategies, a grasp of key data, and the like. (Not to mention funding.) If it doesn't, it'll most likely get its clock cleaned by those who get these things right as the market becomes more competitive.

True, some promising Bright Ideas are doomed by their own creators. A passionate entrepreneur who can't get out of his/her own way is a sadly common tale. But happily a lot of Bright Ideas do succeed: they learn the ropes, get better/smarter, bring in the suits, whatever.

Another familiar story: the Bright Idea succeeds—to the point where it's attractive enough to get bought by a Master. What happens next, too often, is the Master applies what it does best, offering left-brain goodies like scale and efficiency, but also the left-brain downside of standardization, cost-cutting, etc. Not fully understanding or valuing what made the Bright Idea work in the first place, it squeezes the life out of it, turning it into something ordinary. The Bright Idea ends up a shadow of what it could (or may already) have been.

But these are not the only paths. You know where this is heading, right? This is where we talk about the golden square, the magic quadrant, the nirvana place…

An alternate path to success…

For a happy few, there is a fairytale ending.

ICON: The upper-right quadrant is the whole-brain place. Amply endowed with both left- and right-brain savvy, this is the place most brands want to be—for very good reasons.

Icons are brands people actively prefer and choose. Their left-brain mastery allows them to navigate the operational side with skill—but it is their right-brain prowess that wins customers' hearts and loyalty.

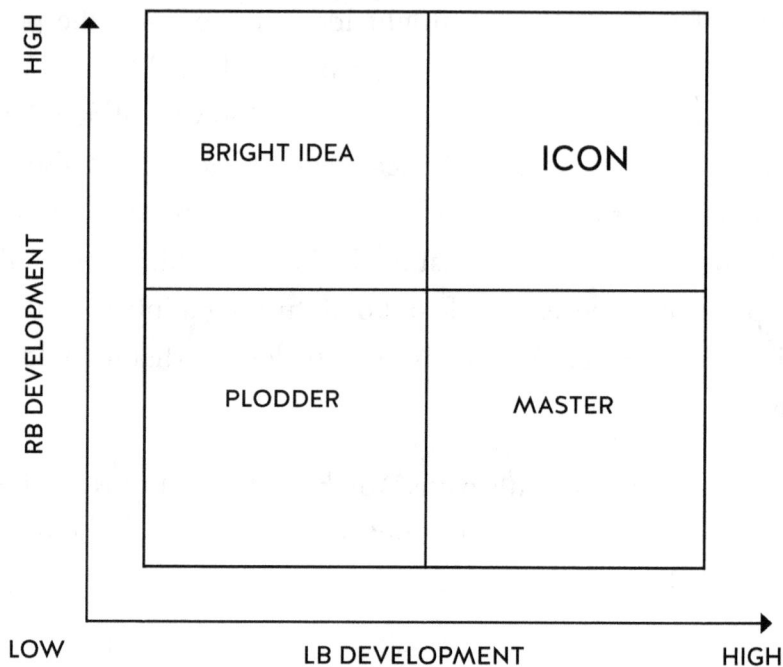

A 2×2 matrix. Vertical axis labeled "RB DEVELOPMENT" ranging from LOW (bottom) to HIGH (top). Horizontal axis labeled "LB DEVELOPMENT" ranging from LOW (left) to HIGH (right).

- Top-left: BRIGHT IDEA
- Top-right: ICON
- Bottom-left: PLODDER
- Bottom-right: MASTER

These are the brands we seek out. We talk about them. We often pay more for them, cheerfully. We don't readily see other brands as substitutes. These brands are part of our lives, and we would mourn them if they disappeared.

Meanwhile, inside the company, something keeps the best people there, and keeps people energized and dedicated. They're less likely to jump ship because there is something special and slightly magical they'd be hard pressed to find elsewhere.

On the next page let's take a look at examples within a single category to bring the matrix to life—then you'll have a chance to apply it.

Putting it all together

The airline industry is a place where we can easily find players of all types. You can plot out the airline category yourself in a more nuanced fashion, of course, adding more players and placing them strategically, not just plunking them in the middle. (You can even make it a bubble chart!) But here's the gist...

PLODDER: Mesa Airlines

A Phoenix-based regional carrier operating flights as United Express, US Airways Express, and under the go! brand in Hawaii, Mesa has figured out a way to survive in a tough, complex market. It doesn't have much of a brand, but it seems to have found a sustainable niche.

MASTER: United

The world's largest airline by number of destinations and scheduled passenger miles, United has weathered most of the bumps for which this challenging industry is known, including its own bankruptcy. Passengers fly United because it meets basic needs (price, schedule, destinations, safety) but it's scarcely a brand that engenders fond feelings and loyalty these days.

BRIGHT IDEA: People Express

A no-frills airline with a simple fare structure, People Express was beloved by passengers for its cheap fares, flexibility, and casual, friendly style. It grew fast—too fast, and not in smart ways. Plunging into financial trouble in a few short years, it was merged into Continental in 1987.

ICON: Southwest Airlines

The world's largest low-cost carrier, Southwest has the best of both worlds. Savvy left-brain strategy shines through its low amenities, short hops, fast turnaround, and single-aircraft focus, but it wins customer loyalty through its big-picture, big-personality, human-centered appeal. Jet Blue has grown to near iconic status through some of the same means, but efforts by major carriers to challenge these two through copycats (United/Ted and Delta/Song) with ersatz friendliness and personality failed miserably.

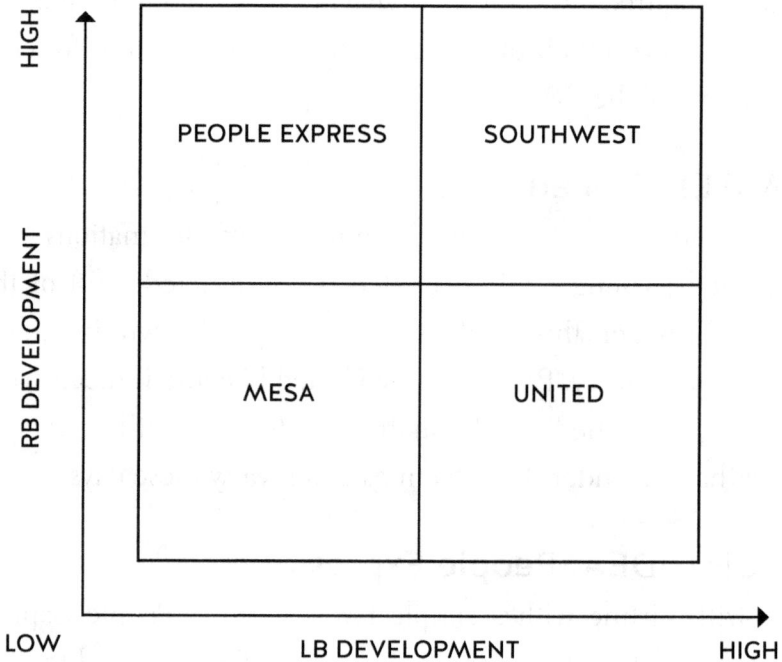

PEOPLE EXPRESS	SOUTHWEST
MESA	UNITED

RB DEVELOPMENT (vertical axis, LOW to HIGH)

LB DEVELOPMENT (horizontal axis, LOW to HIGH)

Your Turn

Okay, now you do it. Draw a 2 x 2 matrix and plot the major players in your category, including your own brand. Where would you place your brand? What about your competitors? Don't worry if you don't know "enough" to categorize brands this way—just try it. If you'd rather wait until you've read the rest of the book, try plotting out another category like insurance, automobiles, etc.

As you consider your LB and RB development, think about a spectrum like this* for each axis:

◄───►
NO WAY   ABSOLUTELY!

LB Development:
To what extent do you (they) use: systems, analysis, standardization, category conventions, and/or consumer stereotypes?

RB Development:
To what extent do you (they) use: originality, authenticity, empathy, emotional range, and/or take creative risks?

Plot your brand anywhere in the four quadrants, then each of your main competitors. Try this exercise again after reading the Six Principles.

*Left-brainers will totally want to quantify/standardize this!

```
HIGH │                          ↑
     │                      ABSOLUTELY!
     │
RB DEVELOPMENT
     │
     │
     ←─────────────────────────┼─────────────────────────→
     │ NO WAY                          ABSOLUTELY!
     │
     │
     │
     │                      NO WAY
     │                          ↓
LOW  └──────────────────────────────────────────
              LB DEVELOPMENT              HIGH
```

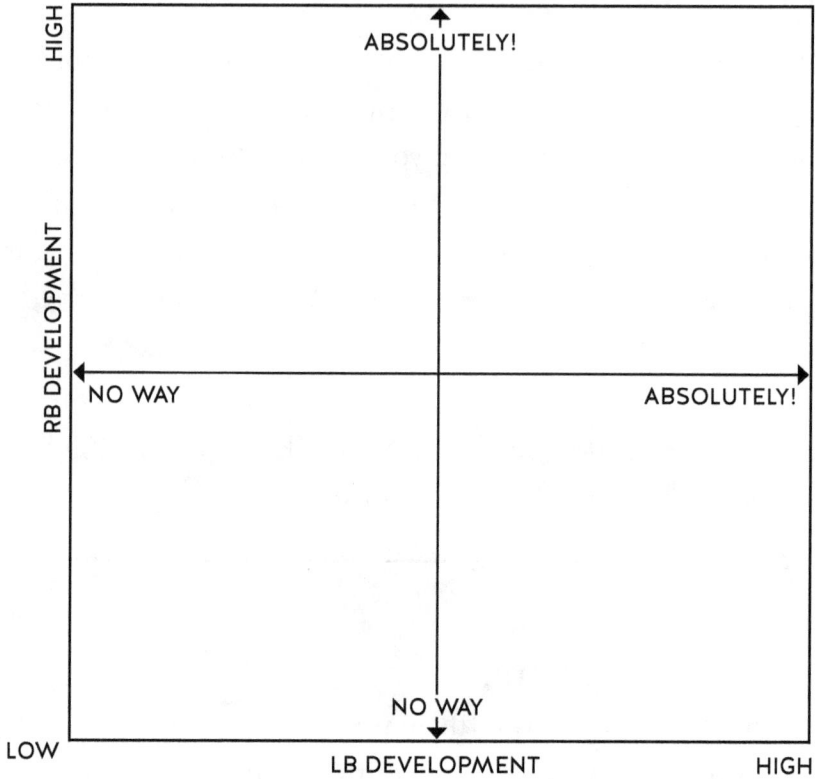

Now the question becomes...

So how *do* you develop right-brain expertise? Ay, there's the rub. There's no single clear, proven, sanctified path.

There is, however, a lot of experimentation going on. It's a very exciting time. Progressive brands (and companies) are trying all kinds of new approaches and bringing in new experts from non-traditional fields. Anthropologists, storytellers, design strategists, and others are being invited in, and they're having an impact.

Successful thought leaders and entrepreneurs are charting new terrain and writing about their discoveries. Consider these titles:

Believe Me (Michael Margolis)

Change by Design (Tim Brown)

Chief Culture Officer (Grant McCracken)

Delivering Happiness (Tony Hsieh)

Enchantment (Guy Kawasaki)

Fascinate (Sally Hogshead)

Likeonomics (Rohit Bargava)

Start with Why (Simon Sinek)

Wired to Care (Dev Patnaik)

Belief, enchantment, happiness, caring... These aren't words you would have found in a business book title ten years ago — even words like design and culture. They're human-centered and largely heart-centered. They speak to new priorities and values. **This is right-brand land!**

These new discoveries and opportunities can also feel confusing. We want to have a context for these pieces, and it's hard. However exciting, interesting, and worthy these new approaches may be, where do you start? Is there some larger pattern to help make sense of it all?

A guide to unleashing your right-brain genius

So glad you asked. Look no further.

This book offers that larger context—a framework for understanding what right-brain development looks like in brands. In other words, how do Icons get to be Icons?

This book also offers a practical guide to developing your own right-brain thinking so you can apply it to your brand/business. You've all got the capability. **You can do this!** It's not just for the IKEAs and Zappos of the world.

The examples that illustrate the core ideas include brands we'd all consider Icons and some smaller gems. All created resonance in the marketplace by engaging directly with these principles—*not by buying their way to the top.*

We genuinely care about certain brands. They're part of our emotional lives. I want more of them out there, including yours. You want that, too.

So come with me. You'll need to learn some things—and unlearn a few, too. As you'll see, it's not just about What You Do. It's at least as much about how you think: about your offering, your customer, your employees, your place in the world.

As you become familiar with the principles, you'll begin to recognize them in other brands you care about. And you'll also find something else: a sense of expansiveness and hope.

The path to real success is not a narrow, sterile one, but one that welcomes—and needs—your whole brain and your full humanity. Are you ready? Onward!

What Great Brands Know
and Use to Make an Impact:

THE SIX
PRINCIPLES

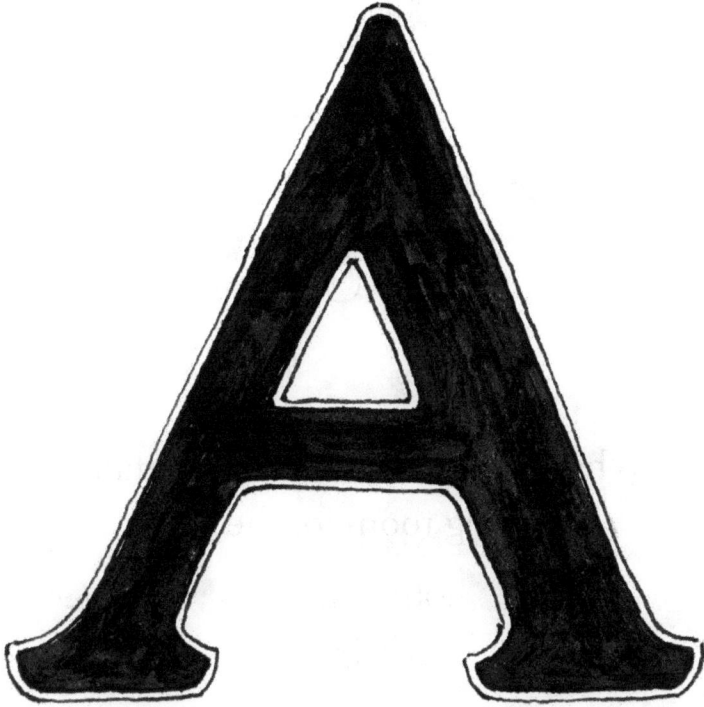

A

IS FOR ART

"

What art offers is space—a certain
breathing room for the spirit.

JOHN UPDIKE

ART

Art in brands and business is about reaching for something timeless that has its own integrity and set of standards.

At some level, Art transcends the commercial realm. And because it does, it's able to find new routes into people's heads and hearts. We are less defended in the presence of Art and more open to enchantment.

Art and Commerce have often been at odds: Art is derided as elitist and impractical, while Commerce is dismissed as crass and utilitarian. But they need not be foes. Today we are absolutely drenched in Commerce. With little Art in our lives, we are more receptive than ever to its charms.

To bring Art and Commerce together effectively requires mutual respect and a shared aim: to create delight for the customer and the world.

In my experience, the key dimensions of Art are: Beauty, Craftsmanship, and The Arts.

"Art isn't only a painting. Art is anything that's creative, passionate, and personal. And great art resonates with the viewer, not only with the creator."
—SETH GODIN

BEAUTY

Pleasing to the aesthetic senses

The sleek contours of a Porsche. The smooth, rich feel of paper in Moleskine notebooks. The elegant design of Apple packaging, which we save for no reason other than its loveliness.

This is Beauty. It attracts us and lights us up inside, creating a moment of glorious sensation around it.

WHAT BEAUTY IS: Beauty evokes admiration and delight for itself, rather than for its uses. It touches both our senses and our soul. It expresses an ideal, which we recognize at some inner level. In a brand, Beauty is intrinsic to what the brand stands for and how it presents itself to the world.

WHAT BEAUTY IS NOT: It's not just about appearance or "pretty." It's not an afterthought, slapped on at the end, a frill outsourced to package designers or the marketing department.

WHY BEAUTY MATTERS: We humans crave Beauty. We're drawn to it. We respond to it both physically and emotionally. And in a world glutted with products and services, Beauty matters more than ever.

Design pioneers like Target, Braun, Herman Miller, and Apple have proven that Beauty through design can provide an enduring edge, distinguishing a brand and merging with people's understanding of it.

We experience Beauty not only through design—or even just visually. Beauty reaches us through our other senses, too, and in wonderful sensory combinations.

When a product or service embraces Beauty, it tells an important story. Not only does Beauty help the brand stand out, it says: "We want you to experience more than pure function. Sensory pleasure is important, too. We want you to take delight in what we're offering."

In the process, Beauty also telegraphs an even subtler message to its customers, saying: "We are not ordinary. We care about larger things than bare-bones sufficiency and effectiveness. So do you. Come join us."

> **"We need beauty in our lives. We're hard-wired for it, and this need has been with us since the earliest human groupings."**
> −ROBERT DALTON

Tea Forté

Tea is more than just a product. Imbued with centuries of tradition across myriad cultures, tea is an experience. From complex tea ceremonies in Asia to rituals of comfort and elegance in the UK and elsewhere, brewing and consuming tea is an important part of culture in much of the world.

For most Americans, though, tea has been a bag plucked from a box and plunked in a cup of hot water. Differentiation centered mainly on what was in the bag (black, green, herbs, etc.) or on the box (e.g. utilitarian Lipton or hippie-groovy Celestial Seasonings). In 2003, former Museum of Modern Art designer Peter Hewitt set out to change this when he started Tea Forté.

"I wanted to create a total sensory and emotional experience that was relevant to life today. I considered taste, smell, touch and, of course, visual presentation. I wanted to create a simple ceremony, a special moment to enjoy with family, friends or just by myself."[1]

Hewitt redesigned virtually everything, aiming to create an absorbing, pleasurable, and engaging experience. Tea Forté bags (known as infusers) are tall nylon pyramids in which high-quality whole leaf tea has room to expand. Unlike traditional tea bags that sink to the bottom of the cup (to be removed by a string or fished out with a spoon), Hewitt's remain upright, topped with a small decorative leaf. Each infuser is boxed in its own distinctive pyramid package. Square ceramic "stages" were developed to host a single bag. Covered cups and teapots featuring a hole in the lid (for the leaf to pop out) were later added.

> *"I didn't know what to expect at that first show. I unwrapped these sculptural works of art, filled with fresh picked teas, herbs and flowers, and placed them on their little green ceramic "stages". They were my babies, and only I knew that I loved them. The response was overwhelming, almost magical. People from all walks of life, and from all corners of the world, felt the same connection and excitement for Tea Forté."[2]*

From these humble, handmade beginnings Tea Forté grew swiftly. Starting with distribution via high-end gift shops, boutiques and gourmet food stores, the brand expanded to elite department stores (Neiman Marcus, Saks Fifth Avenue, Gumps) and then to spas and upscale hotels (Ritz-Carlton, Four Seasons, W Hotels). Growth tapered with the economic downturn (not surprisingly at $1 per infuser), but in 2011 the company generated sales of $12 million. In 2012 it was sold and folded into D.E. Master Blenders 1753 (international beverage division of the former Sara Lee company).

Huge companies have a mixed track record when acquiring small, distinctive brands. Hopefully its new corporate owner will recognize and maintain Beauty as a central, defining feature of this small jewel.

CRAFTSMANSHIP

Quality of design or work; artistry; excellence in execution

Craftsmanship is the quality of "just-rightness." Artistry and care melded with the element of ease. Hard to convey in words, but we recognize it when we experience it. The solid "thunk" as a Mercedes door closes. The felicity of a Jon Stewart one-liner. The careful spareness of the Google homepage. We relax and take delight in the presence of understated expertise.

WHAT CRAFTSMANSHIP IS: Craftsmanship is a form of refinement, which properly blends the two notions: repetition and delicacy. In Craftsmanship we perceive a depth of care, a pride in artistry and skill, a willingness to do the hard work of perfecting something so that we can experience it as effortless.

WHAT CRAFTSMANSHIP IS NOT: Craftsmanship is not a

stylish synonym for "quality." It's not fundamentally about engineering, process, or inputs, though these are certainly vital. "Quality" is often defined in numbers and by subtraction or absence: zero defects, reduction in complaints, elimination of outages. Instead, Craftsmanship is about what is actively present in an experience—what leads to a small inner ping! of joy. It is perhaps most reliably measured by a smile.

WHY CRAFTSMANSHIP MATTERS: Craftsmanship stems from an internal drive to produce something great. Because it is internal, we can count on it. We can count on you. What you offer us is not staged for show. You will do the right thing when no one is looking. You will continue to work on it, gladly. Because you care, because you are slightly obsessed.

Beyond the positive creation of delight, Craftsmanship is a signal that you can be trusted. We would like to believe and accept, but we are wary. We have been burned too often. When Craftsmanship is present, we can both enjoy—and relax.

"If people knew how hard I worked to achieve my mastery, it wouldn't seem so wonderful at all."
—MICHELANGELO

Zildjian Cymbals

In 1618, like many of his fellow alchemists, a young Armenian was trying to create gold from base metals. In the course of his experiments, Avedis, who lived near Constantinople, accidentally created an alloy of copper, tin, and silver that bounced—and when it did, it rang like a bell. He formed this new alloy into cymbals, which at the time were used mostly by the military to create noise with which to intimidate the enemy. The Sultan of the Ottoman Empire, Ossman II, was delighted, and Avedis was given the title of Zildjian ("Master of Cymbals"). He started the Zildjian Company in 1623.

Over time, cymbals based on the family's secret alloy found their way into music, inspiring Mozart and Haydn to incorporate cymbal parts. As the instrument's popularity grew and other companies emerged, later composers like Wagner and Berlioz insisted only Zildjian cymbals be used.

In 1908, Avedis Zildjian III moved to Boston to start a new life. He wanted no part of the 300-year-old family business, which had never been very profitable. But in 1927, as the only surviving male heir to the family's secret formula, he was persuaded to take up the reins. The company was incorporated in the U.S. in 1929—just as the Great Depression began.

It was also the beginning of the Jazz Age. Avedis started visiting Boston's new jazz clubs. As he met with local and visiting drummers, he learned there was a great need for different and better cymbals. Traditional cymbals designed for orchestras were too loud and heavy for drum kits. Drummers' needs were many: a brief dramatic sound that faded quickly, a cymbal to keep time, and more. As Dev Patnaik recounts in *Wired to Care: How Companies Prosper When They Create Widespread Empathy*:

> *"Paying close attention to their performances, Avedis revamped his entire product line to be suitable for jazz music. The resulting creations, the Crash, the Ride, the Splash, and the Hi-Hat, are all staples of the modern drum set. The strategy was so successful that the company was able to build a new factory in the midst of the Great Depression. In 1938, Avedis was featured in Newsweek magazine as one of America's master craftsmen, someone who was prospering despite the economic hard times."[3]*

Armand, Avedis' son, was next in line. According to the company website: "By the time he was fourteen, he had been taught the Zildjian secret process of melting alloys and was skilled in every phase of the manufacturing operation." He also became a drummer himself. Continuing to speak with drummers, he gained new ideas for new cymbals and plunged happily into R&D. He even revamped the centuries-old manufacturing process. His continuing innovation led to wildly successful new products that have become top sellers. According to Armand: *"You have to follow the music and listen to the people who are playing it and learn from them. Then you have to make your product go where they are going."[4]*

At nearly 400 years, Zildjian is one of the oldest companies in the world and remains the undisputed leader in its field. Its success stems from a deep inner sense of artistry and service to its customers—Craftsmanship at its finest.

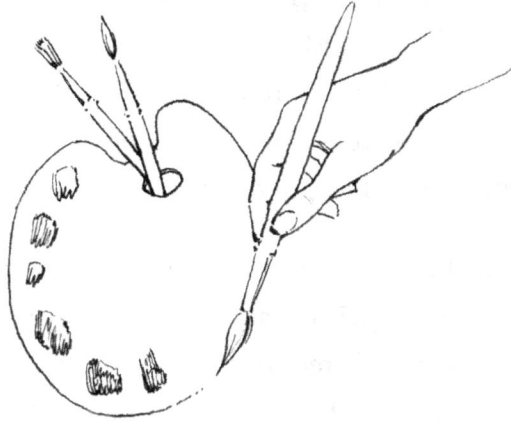

THE ARTS

Purposely using one or more of the branches of creative activity, such as painting, music, or literature

Charles Barkley in a mini-opera for Nike. Haiku in a Target coupon mailer. Iconic black and white photo portraits in Apple's "Think Different" campaign.

WHAT INVOKING THE ARTS IS: A brand deliberately using the Arts steps outside expected industry parameters and embraces originality. It willingly allows us to experience Art first, brand second. It may adapt an existing work of art (or art form) in a new way, or allow individual artistic expression in place of something standardized. Or it may create an original work of art with its own independent merit.

WHAT IT IS NOT: Using the Arts is not gussying up traditional brand-centric activities with a pinch of creative license. It's not an amateur video contest to create the next Pepsi commercial or using trite classical music references (like "Ode to Joy" and "O Fortuna") for background music. Using the Arts for real means taking a risk, with what you do and/or how you do it.

The risk may be slight: so what if the handpainted sign at Trader Joe's is a little sloppy? Yet a commercially-produced sign from HQ carries no risk: it requires no originality and takes no staff time. We respond to the human touch at TJs, and it tells us something about the company.

WHY THE ARTS MATTER: The Arts get noticed when brands use them, in part because they're used so seldom. Yet when we experience the Arts, they touch us in a vital and receptive place. They bypass our well-honed detectors of commercial intent. Instead, they engage our imaginations. Sometimes they trigger a feeling of awe. They allow us to slip, however briefly, into a different world, uniting us with a welcome sense of artistic tradition and community.

Using the Arts in a major, daring way can be quite risky. In 2001-2002, BMW created "The Hire," a series of short films for the Internet by famous directors. Back then, the Internet was a fledgling medium for film at best. "Branded content" had not been invented. Yet beyond making Clive Owen a star, these films caused a cultural sensation, reaching people in ways no product advertising could. Yes, they paid off handsomely, with forty-five million views in two years and sales up seventeen percent the first year alone. At the time this was a real creative gamble, and there were no guarantees.

Sometimes the Arts are perceived as risky because they're considered "elitist," especially arts like classical music and painting. But consider the viral power of classical music flash mobs: opera in a Macy's shoe department, Handel in a food court. Watch the onlookers and you'll see smiling eyes, soft faces, affectionate gestures. Consider how arts festivals and programs have transformed communities and whole cities. Far from elitist, such examples remind us of the power of the Arts to charm and unite us.

Consider this: Google has no commercial reason whatsoever to create its imaginative and playful Doodles. But when it does, the world takes notice and experiences a moment of joy.

"Art is not the bread but the wine of life."
—JEAN PAUL RICHTER

method

Free samples are always terrific, right? Marketing wisdom and common logic converge here. It is a truth universally acknowledged that giving away your new product at no cost is the best way to get people to try it. Next best is to give them a financial incentive, like a coupon or discounted price.

But what if this "truth" is wrong? What if samples and discounts aren't needed—and may end up sullying your brand? What if you could intrigue people enough that they'd try your unknown product—and be willing to pay full price for it?

In a compelling case study, Tom Fishburne, better known as Marketoonist, describes his experience when he launched the method brand in the UK as head of the company's international operations. If you're not familiar with method, it's a line of cleaning products that's a far cry from the standard shelf fare of P & G and its competitors. Stylish clear bottles of minimalist design contain eco-friendly, non-toxic formulations. Launched in 2001, the brand is sold throughout the U.S. and UK, Canada, and Australia with annual revenue of $200 million. (In September 2012, it was sold to, Ecover, a European competitor based in Belgium.)

As the brand explored sampling options in the UK, it quickly discovered that sampling personnel in major retailers treated all brands pretty much the same. It didn't matter if it was a breakfast cereal, a snack food, or a household product. Since the method brand wasn't Just Another Brand, the company sought another route. Working with a local talent agency (Mash), they recruited performance artists who were looking for extra work between acting, singing, and dancing gigs and trained them to represent the method brand. According to Fishburne, the artists took their training as seriously as if it were an acting role. Here's what happened next:

> "Grocery chain Tesco wouldn't let us bring our own samplers, so we focused on DIY retailer Homebase who were more flexible. We even manned a 24-day consumer event called the Ideal Home Show. The performance artists were so persuasive and engaging, we didn't have to give away free samples. Instead, we sold our products for full price at the stand, ultimately selling enough to cover the cost of the show. It was self-funding marketing.
>
> At one point in the show, I spotted a sampling team for Persil, a competitor brand. They stood in the middle of the hall, frantically stuffing free samples into people's over-stuffed bags without a word. It became just another free sample, lost in the clutter. Persil's sampling budget dwarfed ours, but their impact was significantly less."[5]

It's true that method is a distinctive brand. By its very creative, non-conformist nature it's more likely to come up with creative, non-conformist promotional ideas. But it's also true that what passes unchallenged as marketing wisdom can be rote, trite, and hopelessly dull. As method's example demonstrates, using the Arts may cost no more than traditional approaches and possibly far less. What it takes is willingness and imagination. Professional artists (writers, sculptors, actors, musicians, painters and others) have imagination in spades. The willingness is up to you.

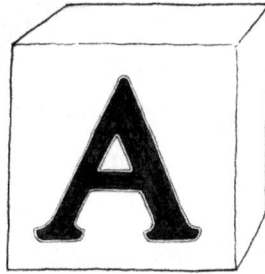

GETTING STARTED WITH ART

Now that you have a deeper understanding of Art and how three remarkable brands have applied it to their own work, products, and messaging, the first step is to get comfortable with these principles yourself. Of course you want to apply them — but there are no cookie-cutter applications. Even an outside consultant can't help you unless you get started on this first.

So start small by trying these experiments and ideas within your company. They'll lead to interesting conversations. After all, it's through conversations that method that was able to come up with its powerful idea. Getting comfortable with these principles will create opportunities for you to apply them to your brands. Enjoy the ride!

Beauty in the everyday

Since we're all familiar with the eye-of-the-beholder factor, developing a broad appreciation for what others consider beautiful can help us expand our collective understanding of Beauty.

- Create a safe space where people within your team (or company) can write or speak about small everyday things they consider beautiful and why. Start generating ideas using sensory experience. In sports, for example, one person may appreciate golf based on all of his/her senses. Another may find aesthetic pleasure in creating a perfectly made bed with fresh-smelling sheets. Sharing ways to find Beauty in the ordinary can heighten our awareness of small things that can make a real difference: to our fellow employees, our customers, and ourselves.

Artists are good at finding Beauty in the familiar. Consider tapping the talents of amateur artists within your workforce. Here's one approach:

- Schedule a photo exhibition on the theme of Beauty and invite all amateur photographers at your workplace to capture Beauty in photos taken on site. Given them some time during work hours in which to do this, and encourage them to explain why they're choosing a specific object or scene to photograph.

Craftsmanship at work

Do people working throughout your company understand what goes into making your products and getting them to customers? Or what care is taken in designing, refining, and executing the services you offer? You will surely find gifted, committed people behind the scenes with great stories to tell—stories that would deepen everyone's appreciation of what your company does.

If your company has resources, professional storytellers can assist you. If not, you can try it yourself at no (or low) cost:

• Enlist a couple of relatively new employees with good communication skills (perhaps English, history, or journalism majors) or approach a local college/university with an internship opportunity. The goal: to interview key, indispensable people throughout the organization and convey their work and expertise through stories in clear, compelling language. Create opportunities to shine the spotlight on unsung heroes in R&D, operations, and elsewhere.

• Who knows? Along the way you may discover some remarkable insights that can help tell the story of your brand in a fresh way. At a minimum, you'll build greater appreciation for the whole of your operation and a greater sense of community.

The Arts and your brand

The goal here is not to produce a deliverable (like advertising), but to stir creative juices and fresh perspectives. Ideas are almost limitless here, but consider the following as thought-starters:

• **Literature:** How could your brand benefits be expressed in limericks, haiku, or sonnet form? How might famous writers (Hemingway? Edgar Allen Poe? Dr. Seuss?) rewrite your ad or packaging copy, or a piece of collateral? Consider a contest with low-cost, imaginative prizes.

- **Visual art:** Invite art students from a nearby college/ university/art school in for a discussion with your brand team. Brief them on your brand and audience, then ask them to respond to what they've heard in a visual medium such as a sketch or collage.

- **Music:** Given the current situation of your brand, what would its theme song be? What about its competitors?

"Art is not delivered like the morning paper;
it has to be stolen from Mount Olympus."
–WAYNE THIEBAUD

B

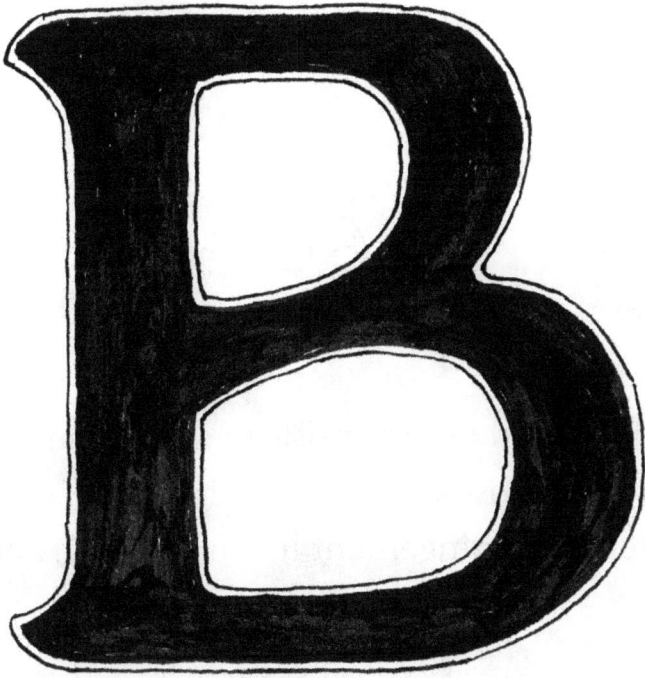

IS FOR BALANCE

66

Genuine good taste consists in saying much in few words, in choosing among our thoughts, in having order and arrangement in what we say, and in speaking with composure.

FRANÇOIS FÉNELON

BALANCE

Balance serves as a counterpoint to the unconscious imbalances pervasive in business and marketing today. Imbalances that sound like this:

Marketing must be Big and Bold!

We must match or outdo the competition!

*We must integrate today's exciting new tactic
into our marketing mix!*

The list goes on. While these phrases are obnoxious to many, we rarely examine or question these underlying assumptions, whether we're head of the marketing department or a small business owner. We operate on autopilot and act upon ingrained beliefs as if they were eternal truths. In the process, we become oblivious to the consequences.

We accept the cumulative results as Just the Way It Is, never mind that it's largely produced a shrill shout-fest, clutter, meaningless feature creep and a pointless arms race of tactics.

Balance is about awareness and choice, both in what we do and how we do it. When we bring awareness to our assumptions and actions, we can choose from a larger range of possibilities. We can make conscious decisions about selecting our marketing elements and integrate them intentionally, rather than zoning out.

For professionals, Balance requires subtlety, discipline, and attention. We must stay constantly mindful, to avoid slipping into easy habits and nostrums.

As consumers, Balance reaches us in a non-intellectual place: perhaps our heart, our body, or our spirit. It is more felt than seen. It may show up as a charming congruence of experience elements. A calm presence amid an onslaught of hype. A welcome sensation of new path-taking. In any of its forms, Balance feels fresh: a relief from sameness and compulsion, and we open toward it.

The three key dimensions of Balance are: Harmony, Equanimity, and Zagging.

"Happiness is not a matter of intensity but
of balance, order, rhythm and harmony."
–THOMAS MERTON

HARMONY

A pleasing integration of elements

Of all the elements of right-brain marketing, Harmony is the most elusive to convey. We experience it mostly in its absence: when we notice something jarring or "off." When we are aware of the pieces. When we feel effort, and the imprint of disparate minds.

When Harmony is present, everything feels whole. It simply works. There is an inner hum. We experience a small sense of well-being, a little uplift.

WHAT IT IS: Harmony is the presence of multiple, mutually re-inforcing elements that work together to create a pleasing whole. Harmony arises from a layered and unified vision of how people should experience the brand.

We experience Harmony when the logo and the copy next to it seem to reflect the same values. When we sense congruent themes and a unifying ethos whenever we engage with the brand.

In brands, as in the word itself, Harmony contains two principal notions: agreement (the parts complement one another) and resonance (evoking a satisfying response).

WHAT IT IS NOT: Harmony is not, "integrated brand marketing." Plenty of brands have well-integrated marketing programs that are unspeakably dull, or even snarky and offensive. Instead, brands with Harmony offer an aesthetically satisfying approach marked by wholeness, proportion, and blend.

WHY HARMONY MATTERS: Harmony creates a subtle, happy totality of feeling. In brands lacking Harmony there is white noise or worse: harshness, friction, and other impediments as we subconsciously process ungainliness or reconcile disparate perceptions. A brand with Harmony, however, occupies a clean, well-lighted place in our minds, a place to which we turn with pleasure and ease.

"With an eye made quiet by the power of harmony, and the deep power of joy, we see into the life of things."
—WILLIAM WORDSWORTH

Prêt à Manger

Prêt à Manger, the beloved British quick-serve sandwich shop (also in select US cities, Hong Kong, and Paris), exemplifies Harmony. Everything works — and works together. From its menu to its employment practices, we sense a thoughtful and unifying presence behind the brand.

Prêt is not the first to focus on fresh, natural foods. But it may well be the first vendor of packaged sandwiches to prepare everything on-site, same day. No additives or preservatives — and no central kitchen. There are no "sell by" dates for a simple reason: anything left at the end of the day is donated to charities working with the hungry.

The Prêt menu is playful, the food delicious. Ingredients are locally and ethically sourced. While fast-food companies often avoid challenging ingredients, such as getting avocados at perfect ripeness, Prêt wears the challenge as a point of pride. In U.S. stores, shop walls are hung with eye-catching posters featuring whimsical, artful food photography and lighthearted brand messaging. Clean, bright shops are well staffed to minimize waiting, with far more registers than, say, a Starbucks. Clive Schlee, the company's chief executive, maintains that Prêt à Manger means "ready to eat, not ready to wait." The goal is to serve each customer within a minute.

Indeed, Readiness is a theme that threads perceptibly throughout the brand. Readiness of ingredients: in how they are sourced (nearby) and offered (at their peak). Readiness of preparation (on-site) and service (now!). Readiness to begin the cycle afresh (no day-old goods). Prêt's Readiness motif creates an energy for the brand, from back room to counter, that contrasts starkly with most quick-serve restaurants that rely on traditional approaches and processes marbled with corporate-slanted slack.

It is no accident to find friendly and enthusiastic employees in Prêt shops. According to a NY *Times* article on the company's employment practices, qualities like "cheerfulness" are used as a basis to hire, pay, and promote, and bonuses are awarded based on team performance.[1] The company also has extensive commitments to social responsibility, from eco-friendly initiatives (e.g. recycling, composting, carbon reduction) to inclusive hiring: in the UK they offer apprenticeships to marginalized citizens, such as people with no fixed address or those with prior criminal convictions.

Collectively, the impact is one of thoughtfulness, care, fun, and outstanding food. Prêt à Manger fully embodies Harmony and challenges the very notion of what fast food is—or can be.

EQUANIMITY

Mental calmness, composure, emotional equilibrium

Think Zen vs. machismo. Invitation vs. exhortation. Implicit vs. explicit.

In brands, think VW Beetle vs. Chevy Camaro. method vs. Tide. Starbucks vs. Dunkin' Donuts.

Marketing is often associated with assertion, hype, and swagger. These qualities align with left-brain thinking, which emphasizes the dominant, active, and worldly. By contrast, right-brain thinking favors the quiet, spiritual, and receptive.

WHAT EQUANIMITY IS: Simply put, brands with Equanimity offer a different energy. There is less brand ego, more room for you and me. Figuratively, they are quieter and more complex.

They credit their audience with greater discernment and don't dwell either on comparison or feature-by-feature, benefit-by-benefit explication.

WHAT EQUANIMITY IS NOT: Equanimity is not false modesty, a subtle superiority claim disguised as an aw-shucks understatement. Nor is it an occasional flirtation with a quieter communications style.

WHY EQUANIMITY MATTERS: Equanimity offers a welcome respite from marketing aggression. By creating a refuge from linearity and hype, it imbues brands with quiet confidence, strength, and depth. Brands with Equanimity offer a more sophisticated emotional appeal. They're more intriguing. And they have more class. Though quieter, brands with Equanimity are more likely to be talked about. They invite us to spread the word because they are not buttonholing us to yammer about themselves.

"Calmness is the cradle of power."
–J.G. HOLLAND

Warby Parker vs. SEE Eyewear

At first blush, these two eyewear companies couldn't be more alike. Both offer exclusive (largely retro) designs—including prescription lenses—at moderate prices. Both target urban hipsters. Both have cause marketing programs. As brands, however, they offer a palpably different energy.

SEE Eyewear

SEE embodies a traditional approach, in which everything about the brand is assertive. A video starts up immediately on the website. Richard Golden, the founder, starts telling his story: how the high cost of prescription glasses led him to source exclusive designs directly. He cracks jokes and coins his own single word to describe the brand: Fashionomic.

In its marketing, SEE Eyewear executes a Cool Brand playbook with relentless fidelity. The brand aims to be hip, and its branding elements are explicit, from the tagline ("Hip without the rip.") to the music soundtrack (jazz—what else?). Company executives are highlighted faux-celebrity style, answering questions about personal background and preferences. The company's cause marketing program, ovarian cancer awareness, features t-shirts and merchandise with an in-your-face quality ("Protect Your Privates") that virtually screams, Aren't We Progressive and Edgy?

Warby Parker

By contrast, Warby Parker embodies Equanimity. There is no soundtrack or video front and center, just a small rotating photo gallery. Where the vibe at SEE is self-congratulatory, bursting with brand ego, at WP it's calm and direct. Where Richard Golden positions SEE (and himself) as a kind of savior to the masses (including his own employees) by eliminating the middleman and lowering prices, WP is simply straightforward: here's the industry, here's what we did, here's what you get. It's even a bit nerdy, complete with a stacked bar chart (the four founders did meet at Wharton, after all).

Where hipness is explicit and ponderous at SEE, at Warby Parker it's tacit and graceful. They have a monocle. Their name comes from two Jack Kerouac characters. Where SEE features execs in glasses as faux celebrities, WP showcases real people (albeit mostly cool young professionals) in a collaborative context: featuring the work of NY photographer who focuses primarily on American youth culture. Their cause-marketing program is a thoughtful, natural fit: for every pair sold, they provide a pair to someone in need by partnering with non-profit organizations like Vision Spring, which trains low-income women to become entrepreneurs, selling affordable glasses in their communities.

In short, SEE is a place where you buy glasses. Warby Parker is also the kind of company you want to tell others about.

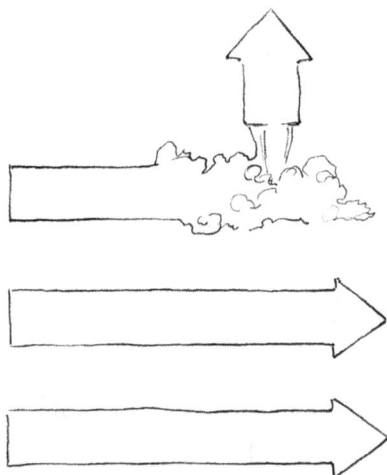

ZAGGING

A counterforce; a sharp change in direction

The final dimension of Balance represents the active embrace of opposition. Brands that Zag are aware of what prevails in their category and consciously choose a different path.

WHAT ZAGGING IS: Zagging means offering a dramatic new approach in a product or service that challenges the established parameters of the category.

WHAT ZAGGING IS NOT: Zagging is not one-upping the competition by offering a major—even quantum—improvement in traditional attributes.

WHY ZAGGING MATTERS: As prominent business authors from Clayton Christensen (*The Innovator's Dilemma*) to Youngme Moon (*Different*) have amply demonstrated, Zagging can have tremendous power, including the power to change markets.

A few compelling examples of Zagging:

Less vs. more: We are used to an endless parade of More in our products. More features, line extensions, options. Where feature frenzy and product proliferation prevail, offering less can slice through the clutter. Flip Video took on camcorder giants Sony and Panasonic by offering…not very much. Yet with a tiny screen, unremarkable picture, a couple of buttons, and no cables (it plugged directly into a USB port), it offered something radical: simplicity and accessibility, and became the top-selling video camera.

Largesse vs. parsimony: Profit pressure (or greed) has led to a trend of shifting costs to consumers. In the process, companies have often cheapened the customer experience as well. Some brands have earned wild success by standing this cheese-paring, line-by-line profit maximization strategy on its head.

While other airlines were trimming amenities, Jet Blue built richness into its experience. Big leather seats and Satellite TV. *And* low fares, which allowed it to compete effectively with other low-cost carriers. In 2012 Jet Blue ranked "Highest in Customer Satisfaction Among Low Cost Carriers in North America" (J.D. Power and Associates)—for the eighth year in a row.

> **"Our wretched species is so made that those who walk on the well-trodden path always throw stones at those who are showing a new road."**
> —VOLTAIRE

IKEA

Swedish-based retailer IKEA has become a huge success by up-ending virtually every standard in the furniture industry. It has created a global powerhouse, filling homes with Swedish design (and stomachs with Swedish meatballs) in thirty-eight countries—not to mention producing a community of millions who know how to wield an Allen wrench. Here are a few of the norms IKEA has reversed:

Furniture lasts: Furniture has traditionally been something passed down from generation to generation. IKEA says, without apology, that its products may not last your first move.

Furniture is expensive: Historically it has taken years to outfit even a room, as you save to acquire one expensive piece at a time. IKEA's low prices may allow you to furnish your home all at once.

Furniture is made by craftsmen: You assemble most IKEA items yourself.

Acquiring furniture is time-consuming: Instead of waiting 4-6 months for delivery, you take it home that day. Wooden items are packed flat in cartons. Limited fabric choices means upholstered furniture is mostly in stock.

Furniture shopping is a big deal: Where most furniture stores are solemn stores visited infrequently, IKEA stores are bright, friendly places where shoppers average 3+ visits/year.

Furniture stores are all about furniture: With a cafeteria and children's play area, IKEA stores have become an outing destination. The IKEA in Shanghai has even become a meeting place for a booming demographic: single seniors 65 and over.

By perfecting the art of Zagging, IKEA has created an extraordinary brand—and become the world's largest furniture retailer.

GETTING STARTED WITH BALANCE

Recognizing and cultivating Balance:

Since Balance addresses prevailing imbalances in brands/ business that are unconscious, our first task is to bring awareness to our automatic assumptions and responses. When we're aware, we can begin to question, see alternatives, and open up a wider range of possibilities.

Harmony

Harmony is subtle and tricky to grasp. One starting point is to consider places where disharmony often occurs, namely during ownership & leadership changes. Set a time to discuss the following situations with your team:

- **Goliath acquires David:** What distinctive, entrepreneurial brands have you seen swallowed up into the maw of a big company only to become something that ends up looking & sounding like everything else? What's been lost?

- **Apple post-Jobs:** Aside from issues of pure technology, what changes have you noticed? Where do/don't they reflect Harmony? How well do these changes bode for Apple's future?

Equilibrium

Equilibrium offers an energy that contrasts sharply with traditional loud, ego-driven marketing. To get familiar with a quieter, less me-focused style, consider the following:

- **Read a book:** Susan Cain's book *Quiet: The Power of Introverts in a World that Can't Stop Talking*, has been a best-seller on every major booklist and was *Fast Company's* #1 Best Business Book of 2012. Read this with your team or a group from your office and discuss your responses to it. For a short-cut version, watch and discuss Susan Cain's TED talk,[2] which has over 5 million views.

- **Take a break:** Challenge yourself and your team to take long stimuli breaks regularly. As part of your next team meeting, encourage your team to turn off their e-mail, smartphones, and other distractions regularly—and set sanctioned hours for this. This is an often-recommended tactic to create quality time to concentrate on important work. But pausing the onslaught of external stimuli will also help you and your colleagues cultivate a better relationship with stillness. As you move past twitchy reactivity and gain comfort with silence, you'll find you're more aware (and less tolerant) of hollow blather—and less likely to inflict it on others.

- **Go feature hunting:** Most brands tout their own marvelous features at every opportunity. Yet few people truly care about the fine points in most categories. What's more, overemphasizing features crowds out other possibilities, including establishing a calmer, more confident, and customer-centered vibe. Review your own and your competitors' marketing communications to assess the role of feature-touting. What do you see? What other approaches might be possible?

Zagging

Of the three dimensions of Balance, Zagging is the most straightforward. Here are a couple of ways to think about Zagging, to open up possibilities for your own brand/business:

- **Painful experiences:** What purchases have you made or considered recently that involved painful or cumbersome processes? Here are some common ones along with examples of Zagging solutions. What other examples can you add, either pain points or Zaggers? What pain points exist in your category?

PAIN POINT	REASON	SUCCESSFUL ZAGGERS
Complexity	Too many options in a category you know/care little about	FlipCam video
Distrust	You fear an aggressive salesperson or fine print	Car Max
Scale	You need or want a little of something, but all you can buy is lots, which you don't want and/or can't afford	iTunes ZipCar CVS Minute Clinic

- **Parameter flouting:** Disruptive innovation often comes from companies that flout established category norms, creating something that's "good enough" by established metrics while offering lower price and/or other attributes. Example: Swiss watches (high quality, high price) vs. Swatch (low price + fashion).

  - Try analyzing two to three product categories, exploring where brands in the category cluster by basic criteria (e.g. size, price, available options, where distributed, purchase method, etc.). What patterns do you see—and what outliers? Do you see any areas ripe for change?

  - What parameters exist in your category that you haven't questioned lately?

"There is music wherever there is harmony, order, or proportion."
—THOMAS HALIBURTON

C

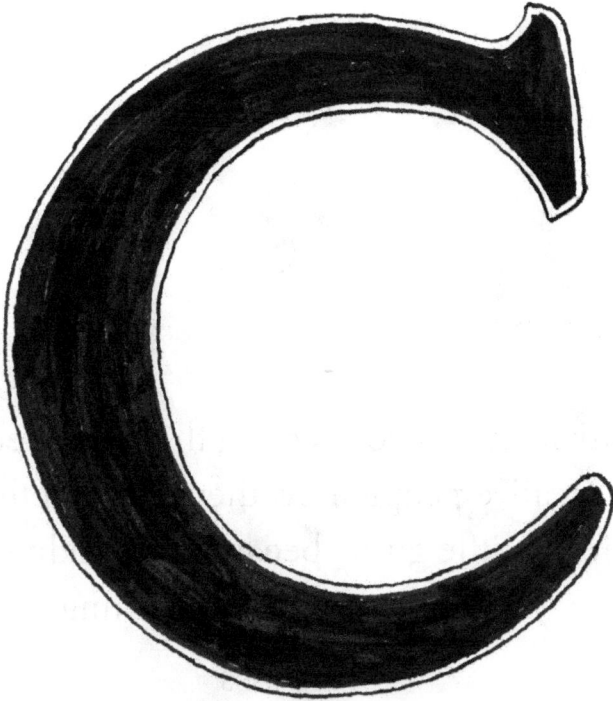

IS FOR
CONNECTING

66

Creativity is just connecting things. When you
ask creative people how they did something,
they feel a little guilty because they didn't really
do it, they just saw something.

STEVE JOBS

CONNECTING

Connecting expresses some of the most familiar aspects of right-brain thinking, ones that stand as polar opposites to the left-brain pillars of logic, linearity, and compartmentalization. These left-brain stalwarts are easy to define—and defend. Their right-brain counterparts? Not so much.

We are constantly challenged to Show Me! Explain It! Prove It! Yet Connecting is about tuning to inner sensations and perceptions—ones that may well resist articulation, much less demonstration or proof.

We all have the raw materials for Connecting, but we may not be conscious of them, much less accord them value. To foster effective Connecting, we must create room within: to become aware of inklings and nonlinear information, and to honor these ideas. Fundamentally, Connecting is an inside job. It's something you allow, rather than an external action you take.

We are so besieged by Show Me! Explain It! Prove It! that we end up censoring our own thoughts. But when we allow ourselves to open to ideas from within and from other settings and sources, we become better listeners, both internally and externally. We begin to hear other things, including a better sense of how things will resonate with customers.

Creating room and permission for Connecting within a company can be a daunting challenge. Of all the six principles of right-brain marketing, it's the one most likely to drive rational left-brainers nuts. Even capturing "it" in words can be difficult, much less offering any proof or justification. Whether it's an intuitive aha!, an illogical combination of key elements, or a hard-to-describe totality, Connecting requires a leap of faith. Yet that leap is what is most likely to take us to a larger, more interesting, and exciting place than the sanctioned, familiar route.

Show me! Explain it! Prove it! These insistences are solid and hard to argue with rationally. Next to these, the fruits of Connecting can feel fluffy and insubstantial. Left-brain challenges can be invaluable at certain times, and they can make us feel more secure, but they are rarely the gateway to magic. Connecting follows mysterious byways, yet it is a far surer path.

The three pillars of Connecting are: Synthesis, Association, and Intuition.

"One of life's most fulfilling moments occurs in that split second when the familiar is suddenly transformed into the dazzling aura of the profoundly new."
—EDWARD B. LINDAMAN, *Thinking in the Future Tense*

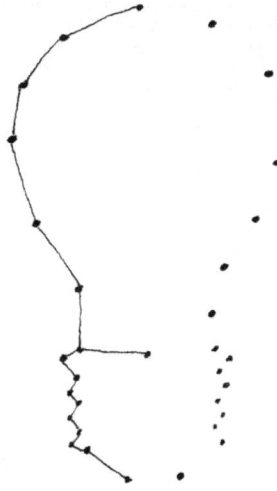

SYNTHESIS

Forming a whole, sensing a pattern, seeing the big picture

Synthesis is what helps us identify emerging ideas, detect and articulate patterns, and create larger and more unified concepts. It is a source of ideas both large and small, from inchoate glimmerings to mature, richly imagined concepts. Brands that abound in right-brain thinking have a gestalt quality: a sense of expansive wholeness that defies item-by-item analysis. Much of this is attributable to Synthesis, where dots are connected to form something unexpected with its own creative integrity.

WHAT SYNTHESIS IS: Synthesis takes many forms. In its most undeveloped state, we may dimly perceive a shape—a sense that ideas are connected in some way for which we can't yet find language. At other times Synthesis may arrive as a metaphor that illuminates a situation in fresh ways. Or we may detect a pattern—

a relationship we can name or demonstrate to others. In its most advanced state, Synthesis allows us to articulate a unified and complex vision.

WHAT SYNTHESIS IS NOT: Synthesis is not accretion, which in brands and business often means the wishful, willful lumping together of ideas to achieve "synergy." Accretion is deliberate and is based on logical, sequential thinking. Instead, Synthesis has a simultaneous, slightly unearthly quality—one that both springs from and is recognized by an inner sense that resists articulation.

WHY SYNTHESIS MATTERS: Synthesis offers us organic brain food vs. the processed products of ratiocination. It allows us to access fresh, nonlinear ideas that are very different from those our rational mind produces. And it helps us give birth and expression to concepts with a resonant sense of wholeness.

"Out of intense complexities intense
simplicities emerge."
—WINSTON CHURCHILL

Banana Republic

Because Connecting is an inside job, we outsiders can't often see where it's taken place. We usually see Synthesis only where it's fully flowered as a richly imagined vision. Rarely can we glimpse those smaller evanescent, aha! moments where ideas take shape.

Happily, Mel and Patricia Ziegler have solved that problem for us. In their book *Wild Company: The Untold Story of Banana Republic*, they give us a remarkable glimpse into Synthesis in action. A journalist and artist, they had no business training whatsoever, but their creative instincts and uncanny understanding of human nature led them to establish one of the most exciting and profitable clothing companies ever. Those who know today's Banana Republic only as the high-end brand in The Gap's company portfolio are really missing something. The original company was remarkable—and a far cry from today's me-too purveyor of business casual clothing.

Synthesis is heralded from the first chapter title: "The Racket Begins with a Jacket." While in Australia for a freelance assignment, Mel discovers a British Burma jacket in a surplus store: "*I had to have it…I wanted to see Patricia's reaction.*" Indeed, Patricia barely recognizes him at the airport—but she's transfixed by the jacket: "*This four-pocket jacket screamed 'authentic' and 'adventure.'*" And on it goes: Mel finds himself repeatedly stopped by strangers who ask where they can get one. They quickly sense the same idea: "*The jacket had a message for me and it didn't take me long to get it: here was the business we'd been looking for.*"

Patricia got the same message on her own. Yes! Between us, we had $1,500 in our bank accounts. We would use it to start a company that would sell jackets like the British Burma jacket and anything else like it we could find."[1]

The vision swiftly takes shape. The name? *"'Banana Republic' popped into my head the moment she asked. What better proverbial source of military surplus than politically unstable tropical countries? I fantasized that routine coups produced an abundance of disposed uniforms from toppled regimes."*[2]

From this initial inspiration, the Zieglers begin selling distinctive, mostly foreign, surplus clothing—much of it "surplus" for a reason. Spanish paratrooper shirts, their first major purchase, all turn out to be short in the arms. No problem—Mel crafts a whimsical story to explain them: *"Defects, I saw, could be worthy sources of inspiration. As for those short-armed Spanish Paratrooper Shirts, the time had come to expose a dirty little secret of history: Generalissimo Francisco Franco's paranoia of long-armed Spaniards. So it went, Andalusian Militia Vests to Ammo Belts. I typed furiously, never missing a chance to dwell on what was wrong... what made the item useless to the army or navy or air force that had declared it surplus."*[3]

Adventure, authenticity, style and whimsy shape their concept, and dots continue to connect. A catalogue, filled with Mel's stories and Patricia's illustrations, resonates with customers all over the country. Stores with a sense of theater (palm trees, jungle animals, colonial ambience) trigger lines out the door. Inspiration strikes again and again. Employees enhance the concept with suggestions. Well-known customers (actors, writers, and others) asked to review clothes for the catalogue respond instantly and enthusiastically: *"The reviews were witty, often hilarious...Uncannily, the reviewers got right into the spirit of the company."*[4]

The company beats all industry metrics for store sales per square foot and catalogue response rates. Don Fisher, Gap founder who acquired Banana Republic, marvels at the cohesiveness of the concept: *"What fascinated him about Banana Republic, as he frequently articulated it, was how we blended merchandise, marketing, and design into a single story; how we named each piece of clothing and wove its tale into the company's ethos."*[5]

Synthesis in action. As expressed by Patricia: *"Henry James claimed that his novels each came from a tiny seed. That is how our line developed. All of Banana Republic's style was seeded in Mel's Burma jacket and the Spanish Paratrooper shirt."*[6]

ASSOCIATION

Linking in idea, making a connection between things

Nonlinear leaps of Association are a trademark of right-brain thinking. Dots are connected in unusual, even contradictory ways. Product innovations resulting from such leaps can become the stuff of legend.

Pouring rubber on a waffle iron, Bill Bowerman created a better running shoe—and co-founded Nike. Visiting Japan, Steve Jobs saw how rice cookers were made safer by using a magnetic power cord attachment—and the magsafe for the Mac was born.

WHAT ASSOCIATION IS: Association is the connecting of two (or more) ideas that may appear to be unrelated at first blush. We tend to view Association as something that arises in a Eureka moment, a serendipitous new perception. But Association can also be sought out deliberately and systematically. In the technical arena, for example, the company Gen3 Partners scouts for potential solutions by looking methodically across a wide range of unconnected industries.

WHAT ASSOCIATION IS NOT: Association is not about relationships of dependence or interdependence (e.g. causation or correlation) that may explain existing phenomena. Instead, it is about recognizing a fundamental connection between ideas in disparate realms that results in something new.

WHY ASSOCIATION MATTERS: Association can lead to breakthroughs of all kinds. Cutting-edge design combined with low prices, for example, has become a core element of Target's brand.

Unlikely hires: Most high-growth software firms fight over the same limited pool of hot young developers. When inbound marketing powerhouse HubSpot needed to scale, it sought out (wait for it) middle-aged big-company engineers, precisely the people routinely dismissed as obsolete, entitled benchwarmers. By seeing past tired stereotypes, HubSpot realized it could get great people with the experience and "flight hours" it needed—and even paid a bonus for each year of experience.

"Creativity is the power to connect the
seemingly unconnected."
—WILLIAM PLOMER

Ben and Jerry's

Of all the innovations for which ice cream pioneers Ben Cohen and Jerry Greenfield are known, their flavors and flavor names are the most famous. Playful and imaginative, Ben & Jerry's ice creams have offered offbeat ideas since the company's founding in 1978.

What makes their ice creams so distinctive is Association: connecting disparate things to form a new creative whole. Ben & Jerry's has used two key types of unconventional linkages, sometimes simultaneously:

Ice cream + cultural references:
• **Music:** Cherry Garcia, Phish Food, Dave Matthew's Band "Magic Brownies," Bohemian Raspberry

• **Pop Culture:** Wavy Gravy, Vermonty Python, Bonnaroo Buzz, Imagine Whirled Peace

• **TV:** Festivus, Schweddy Balls, Late Night Snack, Stephen Colbert's Americone Dream, Taste the Lin-Sanity

• **Politics and the Economy:** Economic Crunch, Yes, Pecan!

Unexpected ingredient and flavor combinations:
In our mature, hyper-extended market, many of Ben & Jerry's innovations seem like standard fare today. At the time, however, many of their signature flavors were considered remarkable, like

Cherry Garcia and Chunky Monkey. Even today, a few of their flavors retain their edge:

• **Chubby Hubby:** With fudge-covered peanut butter-filled pretzels

• **Late Night Snack:** Features fudge-covered potato chips

When Ben & Jerry's was acquired by Unilever in 2000, terms of the agreement specified it would be operated separately from Unilever's other ice cream brands (like Breyers). The company founders no longer play any role in the company, but unlike many other innovative small companies acquired by global giants, Ben & Jerry's continues to maintain its distinctiveness, including its tradition of quirky flavors and social engagement. For example, for the month of September 2009, Chubby Hubby was renamed Hubby Hubby to celebrate the legalization of same-sex marriage in the company's home state of Vermont.

INTUITION

Inner knowing or insight, often of a sudden nature; inspiration

Intuition is a type of inner cognizance. Synthesis and Association are about connecting dots in different ways to form new ideas, but Intuition reflects something else. Consider the following types of "connecting":

Physical: Plugging into an electrical or communications system

Athletic: Hitting a ball solidly or successfully

Social: A sense of mutual resonance

Creative/Spiritual: Tuning into inner guidance

In each of these we sense a sparking quality: a force that goes beyond the ordinary self. It may be a moment of personal insight or a non-verbal understanding between people.

WHAT INTUITION IS: Intuition is non-rational knowing. It often arises as a sudden flash of understanding or insight, but it may also take a subtler form, as a gentle prompting or inner voice.

WHAT INTUITION IS NOT: Intuition is not a snap judgment based on personal bias or preference. Instead it has a transpersonal, quasi-universal quality.

WHY INTUITION MATTERS: Intuition can be a potent source of ideas and information unavailable through other means. At its best, Intuition offers us wisdom. It can generate major breakthroughs. It can also save time and money by providing a shortcut through traditional paths and processes.

In business, however, Intuition is mostly viewed with deep suspicion, though it's tolerated as a necessary evil in creative professions such as advertising and entertainment.

Business prefers ideas drawn logically from reputable sources, such as data analysis, behavioral observation, etc. So in most business settings, Intuition has about as much credibility (and is about as welcome) as a shaman at a hospital: a disreputable throwback to a primitive era that has no place in a modern institution.

Dismissing Intuition out of hand is a mistake, however, because well-developed Intuition can be an extraordinary resource. This does **not** mean all intuitive ideas are necessarily good, much less commercially viable. But it **does** mean that Intuition can play an important role. The wisest brands and business leaders view Intuition as an ally: a wellspring of insight that offers great potential for ideas and guidance.

"I believe in intuition and inspiration... At times I feel certain I am right while not knowing the reason."
—ALBERT EINSTEIN

Steve Jobs

Steve Jobs had profound respect for Intuition, which played a major role throughout his life and work. Here are a few instances where the role of Intuition is explicitly discussed in Walter Isaacson's excellent biography, *Steve Jobs*. *(Direct quotes from Jobs in italics.)*

Eastern influences

Buddhism: "Jobs also became deeply influenced by the emphasis that Buddhism places on intuition. *'I began to realize that an intuitive understanding and consciousness was more significant than abstract thinking and intellectual logical analysis.'"*[7]

India: "*Coming back to America was, for me, much more of a cultural shock than going to India. The people in the Indian countryside don't use their intellect like we do, they use their intuition instead, and their intuition is far more developed than in the rest of the world. Intuition is a very powerful thing, more powerful than intellect, in my opinion. That's had a big impact on my work.*"[8]

Product design: Jony Ive, Apple's chief designer, discusses why a handle was designed into the original iMac, the company's innovative jewel-colored computer (1998).

"*Back then, people weren't comfortable with technology. If you're scared of something, then you won't touch it. I could see my mum being scared to touch it. So I thought, if there's this handle on it, it makes a relationship possible. It's approachable. It's intuitive. It gives you permission to touch.*

It gives a sense of its deference to you. Unfortunately, manu-facturing a recessed handle costs a lot of money. At the old Apple, I would have lost the argument. What was really great about Steve is that he saw it and said, 'That's cool!' I didn't explain all the thinking, but he intuitively got it. He just knew that it was part of the iMac's friendliness and playfulness."[9]

On Intuition vs. technology: *'When I went to Pixar, I became aware of a great divide. Tech companies don't understand creativity. They don't appreciate intuitive thinking, like the ability of an A&R guy at a music label to listen to a hundred artists and have a feel for which five might be successful...I'm one of the few people who un-derstands how producing technology requires intuition and creativ-ity, and how producing something artistic takes real discipline.'"*[10]

Bill Gates on Steve Jobs

"Jobs was a 'natural in terms of intuitive taste.' He (Gates) recalled how he and Jobs used to sit together reviewing the software that Microsoft was making for the Macintosh. 'I'd see Steve make the decision based on a sense of people and product that, you know, is hard for me to explain. The way he does things is just different and I think it's magical. And in that case, wow.'"[11]

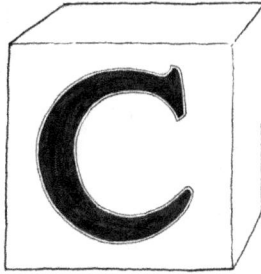

GETTING STARTED WITH CONNECTING

Connecting is an inside job that's rarely valued explicitly in the workplace, so it makes sense to start at home, developing your skills privately first. As you begin to gain confidence in your ability to access and trust various forms of inner, nonlinear guidance, you can begin to take your ideas to work and test them there. The methods below for developing Connecting are actually pretty fun, too.

Synthesis in the everyday

Activities aimed at developing your facility for symbolic thinking are enjoyable—and can be illuminating.

BECOME A METAPHOR DETECTIVE: What are the metaphors in your life telling you? Consider things that have happened recently that are a bit out of the ordinary. What might they mean metaphorically? (Note: If you experience a strong sense of resonance, that's your Intuition talking, pointing you to some inner information that merits further attention.)

Personal example:

You just got a parking ticket for the first time in years. Literally, it means you stayed too long somewhere and didn't put enough money in the meter. Metaphorically, it may have multiple meanings. For example:

• Have you been stuck and zoned out on something specific (or in your life in general) lately?

• Where are you not properly "feeding the meter?" Are you skimping on something routine but important, like self-care and maintenance? What needs more attention and generosity in your life right now?

Business example:

One of your products has inexplicably caught the attention of a blogger. For better or worse, there's social media brewing around it. Literally, it means someone stumbled across your offering and you need to deal with the attention it's causing (whether an opportunity or problem). Metaphorically, what might it mean?

• You've overlooked something that is creating resonance (or dissonance). Do you need to improve your listening skills? Reconsider how you define your audience? Become more careful or intentional overall?

• Is your company near a tipping (or boiling) point with people you haven't been paying attention to, perhaps inside your organization? Could you benefit by seeking feedback from unexpected sources?

TAKE A WALK: Walking a labyrinth is a fun, unconventional activity that you (with or without your team) may be able to try, depending on your location. Labyrinths are maze-like structures dating back to Greek mythology. Today, most labyrinths are unicursal, with a single path leading to the center (vs. mazes, which have lots of wrong turns and only one correct route).

- See if there's one nearby by checking www.labyrinthlocator.com.

- Enter the labyrinth and walk very slowly in silence, tuning out mental chatter and outside stimuli as much as possible. (Keeping your eyes down and half-closed can help.) When you reach the center, pause for a moment, then follow the path back out at the same pace as on the way in.

- After completing the walk, reflect on what images, ideas, and associations came to you during the course of your walk. What did the experience of following an indirect, circuitous path feel like?

Association in the everyday

These games are designed to develop your flexibility in making associative connections between seemingly unrelated things and may be suitable to try at work now, especially if you're working to develop more creative, offbeat ideas.

APPLES TO APPLES ("The Game of Hilarious Comparisons"): Players are dealt Red Apple cards, which feature a word with a person, place, thing, or event. One player (the Judge) draws a Green Apple card with an adjective on it, and places it face up.

The remaining players select a card from their hands representing the best match. The Judge decides which noun is the best match for the adjective. Most of the noun/adjective pairings are ridiculous, and that's the point. But it's remarkable how adeptly the mind works to try to find connections, even absurd ones, between completely random things.

SIX DEGREES OF...: A variation on the well-known game "Six Degrees of Kevin Bacon," where movie knowledge is not required. Pick two words at random from a dictionary. Using imagination alone (no research), try to find the shortest path of connection between the unrelated words.

Intuition in the everyday

These techniques work best if you take the time to consciously quiet mental chatter beforehand. Some are better shared with your team than others—you know best.

ASK A QUESTION: You can do this alone or enlist your team's help, too. Consider a business question you're grappling with. Hold that question in your mind before going to sleep. Don't think logically, just think of the question quietly or write it down. In the morning, ask the question and see what pops into your mind. The result may be an image, a phrase (or, nothing). Try this every day for a while and see what happens. This is also something to try before a quiet non-mental activity like walking, running, yoga, or meditation.

TAP YOUR BODY WISDOM: Here are two methods to deal with binary questions (yes/no, stay/go, etc.). One is fairly traditional, the other a bit unconventional.

GUT CHECK: If you've maxed out on thinking (weighing the pros/cons, etc.), go to a quiet place and just focus on your breathing for a minute or two. Then flip a coin for the answer. Note your immediate physical and emotional response to the choice you made arbitrarily. What do you feel? Joy? Relief? Tension? Regret? The classic suggestion to "sleep on it" is a time-honored variation. Make a decision the night before, then check in the morning for your immediate reaction.

ARM RESISTANCE TEST: Enlist a partner for this. Hold your arm straight out to the side. Have your partner push down gently on your arm while you try to resist and keep your arm up. Then try the push & resist exercise as you answer true/false or yes/no questions. First, start with a basic True question such as: "My name is (your name)." Your partner should not be able to push your arm down easily as you resist. Then try a False response: "My name is (someone else's name)." Your partner should be able to push your arm down easily despite your resistance. Calibrate the pushing/resisting till you get the hang of it, then try the exercise with other questions.

"Trust yourself. You know more than you think you do."
–BENJAMIN SPOCK

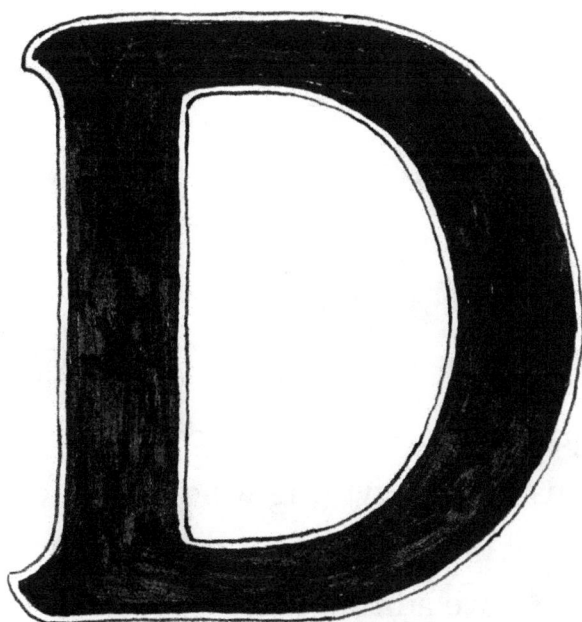

D

IS FOR DEPTH

"

Depth roots us in the world, gives life substance and wholeness. It enriches our work, our relationships, everything we do. It's the essential ingredient of a good life and one of the qualities we admire most in others.

WILLIAM POWERS
Hamlet's Blackberry

DEPTH

We experience Depth in business primarily by its absence—there just isn't much out there. When it comes to touching our essential humanity, the commercial world is a micron deep. Most brands are relentlessly superficial, from how they understand and envisage their customers (much less their own purpose), to how they communicate. More broadly, the true ambit of most businesses rarely extends beyond the immediate world of shareholders and customers. If/when they deign to focus (or sprinkle largesse) elsewhere, this too is most often done shallowly.

Is it reasonable to expect more? Well, reason isn't the issue here. Our purpose is to explore those non-rational elements that make a genuine difference, enabling us to stand out and make people care. Depth offers us huge untapped opportunities in this regard. As you read, you may recognize and appreciate these elements intuitively even if you may not yet have language for them.

Depth is demanding. It requires more from us than business usually asks—or wants. We must be willing and able to go below the convenient shiny surface in which we usually dwell at work. The skeptical, hard-nosed, and risk-averse are unlikely even to understand, much less welcome efforts to bring Depth to our brands and business initiatives. In fairness, many earnest brands brimming with Depth and other right-brain goodies have crashed and burned because they failed at left-brain basics. In these cautionary tales, Depth is often one of the easiest targets for finger pointing. And surely, Depth alone won't make a brand or business succeed.

Yet Depth ultimately offers a more reliable and resilient connection to people than the sanctioned superficiality and tactics *du jour* of traditional business and marketing. Depth through connecting to a larger purpose gives brands sonar power, helping both to navigate and to communicate below the surface. A more richly textured view of humanity can reveal new opportunities and engage everyone more deeply. Discovering and communicating rootedness through story can provide durable points of connection no competitors can touch.

Sure, there are risks, but remaining on the surface offers risks as well—and fewer true rewards.

Depth has three dimensions: Essence, Multidimensionality, and Roots.

"We are already the most over-informed,
under-reflective people in the history of civilization."
–ROBERT KEGAN & LISA LAHEY
Harvard psychologists

ESSENCE

Core purpose or mission

At its core, what is your brand really about? What is its highest and best purpose?

Essence has perhaps been most famously articulated by Steve Jobs. When recruiting John Sculley from Pepsi, Jobs challenged him, asking: *"Do you want to spend your life selling sugared water, or do you want a chance to change the world?"*

To get at Essence you must look past easy answers of features and benefits. You might also have to hack through levels of hype and puffery. If you're lucky, you'll find something beyond sugared water (or its equivalent).

WHAT ESSENCE IS: The gold you seek is simple. At its core, Essence is a sense of service. What are you privileged to be bringing to the world? How are people's lives made better by what you do? How are you an instrument of a larger purpose?

WHAT ESSENCE IS NOT: Essence is not your Mission Statement. Nor is it your worldly context: making money, employing workers, or even contributing to your community, though these are all important.

Instead, Essence is a sense of true purpose, something that connects with fundamental human needs and yearnings. As Steve Jobs would say, it is the ding you're trying to put in the universe.

WHY ESSENCE MATTERS: As humans, we crave meaning. From Maslow's hierarchy to the Dalai Lama's superstar status to the tidal wave of books on spirituality and self-discovery, the quest for meaning is gaining traction in the public sphere.

Brands that authentically embrace meaning through their Essence are able to distinguish themselves and find genuine resonance with their audience. Companies like Patagonia and TOMS Shoes center their brand around their Essence and inspire loyalty in their core customers. With some other companies, you may have to dig a bit deeper, but you can sense when it's present—or not.

Essence can also galvanize morale and effort within the company, and provide a serious edge in attracting and keeping top talent. When we feel part of a grander endeavor, something that improves the world just a bit, our hearts show up as well as our minds and bodies, and we are pumped. There is wind in our sails and a continuing reason (and desire) to do our best.

"Many persons have a wrong idea of what constitutes true happiness. It is not attained through self-gratification but through fidelity to a worthy purpose."
−HELEN KELLER

Costco

Walk into any of Costco's nearly 450 locations in the U.S. and you'll experience a true no-frills warehouse environment, where village-sized packages of rice and toilet paper coexist peacefully alongside fine wines and elite clothing brands. Bargains abound, but it's a mistake to think that's what Costco is all about.

Many companies, most famously Walmart, focus on low prices — but care nothing for their employees. Others like Whole Foods, treat their employees well, but don't necessarily pass along savings to their customers. Costco does both, combining a deep sense of service to customers and employees in a distinctive Essence that defies market wisdom — and regularly irritates Wall Street.

According to Jim Sinegal, Costco's legendary co-founder and longtime CEO, "The traditional retailer will say: 'I'm selling this for $10. I wonder whether I can get $10.50 or $11.' We say: 'We're selling it for $9. How do we get it down to $8?'"[1] In a *Seattle Times* article he asked: "'Who the hell's going to notice if you charge $14.99?' instead of $12…'Well, we're going to know. It's an attitudinal thing — you always give the customer the best deal.'"[2] To enforce its low prices, Costco limits the markups on its products: no branded item can be marked up by more than 14 percent and no private label item by more than 15 percent. This transparency delights customers but isn't popular with Wall Street, which also criticized the company for adding staff at checkouts to shorten lines. Said one analyst, "It was spending what could have been shareholders' profit on making a better experience for customers."[3]

Costco also treats its employees well—too well, to many industry analysts. Starting at an average $11.50/hour, employees earn $19.50 after five years and get an "extra check" of $2,000 every six months. Dubbed "the anti-Walmart" by some observers, Costco also offers generous health benefits for the industry and has good relations with its union employees (roughly 13% of warehouse workers are Teamsters). Costco's high-wage strategy creates a large expense for salaries, but also results in high loyalty and productivity. Turnover after the first year is 6 percent—vs. roughly 50 percent at Walmart, the largest U.S. employer. "Inventory shrinkage" (pilferage by employees) is virtually nil. Friendly, knowledgeable employees make the shopping experience a pleasant one.

Costco's egalitarian streak extends to executive compensation as well. "I just think that if you're going to try to run an organization that's very cost-conscious…having an individual who is making 100 or 200 or 300 times more than the average person working on the floor is wrong,"[4] says Sinegal, whose base pay was $350,000 (though stock ownership made him a very wealthy man). His successor, Craig Jelinek, earns $650,000. By Fortune 500 standards (Costco is #24) this is still an exceptionally low salary.

However unorthodox for American business, Costco's values-based Essence is extremely successful by any measure. For the past two calendar years Costco stock outperformed its peer group even as the peer group significantly outpaced the S&P 500 index. In 2013 to date, same store sales are much higher than both Walmart and Target. Nearly 37 million primary cardholders pay $55/year for the privilege of shopping there ($110 for an Executive Membership), with renewal rates nearly 90% and growing.

MULTIDIMENSIONALITY

A holistic and nuanced view,
especially regarding people

Marketers have been trained to simplify. We opt for broad and shallow vs. narrow and deep. We speak of "the consumer." Packaged goods marketers are not far off when they joke about their target audience as "adults over twenty-five with a pulse."

WHAT IT IS: Multidimensionality is a holistic and nuanced way to look at human beings, one that invites us to embrace quirks and contradictions. Multidimensionality comes from a lively, genuine, and multifaceted interest in human nature in all its intriguing permutations and complexities.

WHAT IT IS NOT: Multidimensionality is not a multivariate approach to data gathering and analysis. While rich, useful data are almost certain to emerge from a Multidimensional stance, data are not the point—people are. Our intent in Multidimensionality is not to reduce people to data we can understand and manipulate, but to understand whom we can delight and how.

Neither does Multidimensionality mean using personas (avatars representing customer segments, often derived from behavioral data), which have become popular in recent years among marketers and product developers. While personas may help optimize user interface on websites, they rarely work as well for new products and services. Why? Because the personas used as inputs are usually clichéd, utilitarian, and tidy, resulting in variations on the ho-hum. They smooth off the rough edges and contradictions that make people real. Avatars may be constructed with layers of details—but they're all hollow generalities, resulting in cardboard cutouts no one would recognize in real life. They rarely lead to anything that will astonish and enchant.

WHY MULTIDIMENSIONALITY MATTERS: A reductionist approach to customer understanding is practically irresistible. Simplifying and compartmentalizing is convenient and often explains a lot. It helps us focus and articulate our offerings, strategies, and communications. But it can come at a steep price, starting with a false sense of clarity and connection.

Few companies eagerly embrace human complexity. Those that do, however, reap big rewards. In an ever more saturated and fragmented marketplace, Multidimensional brands are more distinctive and resilient. They stand out by offering something intriguing that can't readily be replicated. We feel more connected because they "get us," and we reward them with our loyalty. They just feel more interesting, so we're more likely to talk about and recommend them. The "je ne sais quoi" of Multidimensionality translates straight to the bottom line.

"The key to growth is the introduction of higher dimensions of consciousness into our awareness."
—LAO TZU

Trader Joe's

With over 400 stores (in 38 states and DC), Trader Joe's is a familiar destination to many customers—and many more would dearly love it to be. According to a 2010 *Fortune* Magazine article (a rarity, researched without help from the obsessively secret company), "strip-mall operators and consumers alike aggressively lobby the chain...to come to their towns." Why? Because "a Trader Joe's brings with it good jobs, and its presence in your community is like an affirmation that you and your neighbors are worldly and smart."[5]

"Worldly and smart." These are not tip-of-the-tongue adjectives most grocery chains would use to describe their customers. Then again, TJ's isn't most grocery stores. Currently one of the hottest retailers in the United States, it owes much of its success to a thoughtful, multifaceted way of thinking about people.

Founder Joe Coulombe developed a chain of traditional convenience stores for Rexall Drug Co. in Southern California in the 1950s and '60s until pressure from 7-Eleven caused Rexall to exit the category. Inspired by an extended Caribbean vacation, Coulombe bought out the stores and embarked on a new strategy. Recognizing that consumers were becoming more sophisticated and well-traveled, he decided to focus on a well-educated but not necessarily wealthy audience. As he told *Forbes* in 1989, he saw his customers as people "like teachers, engineers, and public administrators. Nobody was taking care of them."[6] He opened his first Trader Joe's in 1967 in South Pasadena, expanding in the region by targeting communities where state colleges/universities were beginning to bloom.

In its early years, Trader Joe's responded nimbly to economic and regulatory changes, evolving to offer a unique merchandise mix that continues to this day: upscale, value-oriented beer and wine along with unique food products that are often imported and mostly private label. Today's TJ's stores carry specialty foods like Thai lime-and-chili cashews and mango passion granola as well as high-quality, often organic staples—all at rock-bottom prices. Where beer and wine sales are allowed, wines priced $10-$20 keep company with "two-buck Chuck" (Charles Shaw wines).

Part of TJ's' Multidimensional genius is recognizing consumers' inherent contradictions. We pair an adventurous gourmet meal of exotic ingredients with two-buck Chuck. We buy no-name staples but may spring for a $100 bottle of wine. We crave comfort foods like mac & cheese and rice pudding but also want novelty and excitement: mochi ice cream (Japanese) and Balela salad (Middle Eastern).

Multidimensionality extends to employees, too. TJ's offers its Hawaiian shirt-clad staff high wages and generous benefits, a rarity in the industry. Full-time "crew members" (store employees) start at $40K-$60K; managers can make in the low six-figures. TJ's ranked #9 in Forbes' Best Places to Work in 2011. Staff members cheerfully accept returns without question—or receipts—and are likely to escort you to find an item you're looking for. They ask about your favorite products and share their own recommendations.

This unconventional approach has been hugely successful. Owned since 1979 by Germany's ultra-private Albrecht family (which owns European supermarket giant Aldi Nord), TJ's generates an impressive $8 billion/year in sales, equivalent to all of Whole Foods, with double the sales per square foot. Stocking only 4,000 SKUs (less than 10% of a typical supermarket), stores nonetheless feel like places of abundance and discovery. Multidimensionality has helped this offbeat business flourish, creating a thriving, growing chain where every store feels like a homey, neighborhood place.

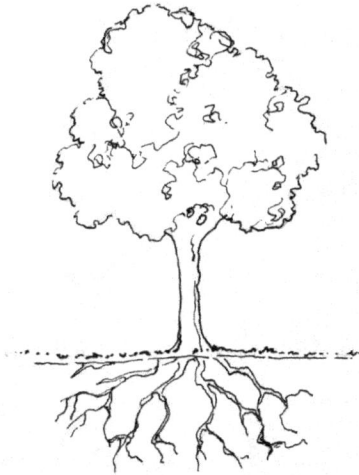

ROOTS

Deep sources of nourishment and vitality conveyed through story

From the celebrated preferences of cultural luminaries to tales of fabled garage startups, we love the stories that surround brands. Certain kinds of stories give a brand Roots, linking us to larger worlds of time, place, and meaning—while also helping craft our own tastes and choices.

WHAT ROOTS ARE: Roots are what give brand or company Depth by anchoring it authentically to something outside the brand that has its own integrity: history, geography, symbolic meaning, and the like.

We can understand Roots by looking at different types of terrain that serve as the source for both brand nourishment and compelling stories. Here are a few classic examples:

Origins: By now, who hasn't heard how Post-It® notes were invented? The creation tale of the failed adhesive used on slips of paper to mark a hymnal has become legend.

Heritage: Today Harley-Davidson's customers are more likely to be middle-America boomers than scruffy outlaws, but Harley's historic link with Hells Angels and edgy iconoclasts ("Easy Rider") continues to fuel its badass image and appeal.

Archetypes: From poking fun at competitors' absurdities (like baggage fees and blackout dates), to the humor and personality of its staff, Southwest Airlines embodies the Jester archetype. This intuitive storyline resonates naturally and helps reinforce the brand's distinctiveness.

Roots offering brand nourishment can also include elements like geography, cause-related community (when aligned with Essence), ethnicity, and more.

WHAT ROOTS ARE NOT: Roots are not self-serving brand stories orchestrated to create the perception of popularity. Though brands may covet—and strive to engineer—"grassroots" cred via ripples of social media attention (the viral video, the crowdsourced ad) these efforts have all the naturalness (and enduring appeal) of AstroTurf.

Faux Roots: Some successful lifestyle brands (like Tommy Bahama and Hollister) are built around entirely fictitious characters. While these and other trend-surfing examples may become quite profitable, their customer loyalty is far shallower than to brands with authentic origins, and they are more vulnerable to shifting winds of taste.

WHY ROOTS MATTER: Roots help brands by offering points of connection that transcend the purely commercial realm. Beyond helping shape brand image, they make the brand feel larger and more substantive, giving us reasons to choose and prefer it. They help establish and sustain authenticity, creating resonance with customers and sources of meaning within the company. For example:

- Creation stories are inspiring and can often be a touchstone for refocusing when a brand or company loses its way.

- Heritage stories reflecting who has engaged with the brand over time (along with how, where, when, and/or why) help connect the past with the present and future. We want to be part of a larger story and longer timeframe.

- Archetypal stories connect with universal themes hardwired into human beings and provide shortcuts to meaning, leveraging storylines we already understand and value.

Like a plant, brands are more likely to flourish when they have well-developed Root systems: multiple areas of connection that also go deep. And, as with plants, Roots like these can help brands weather tough conditions of drought, storm, and disaster.

"Storytelling reveals meaning without committing
the error of defining it."
–HANNAH ARENDT

Moleskine Notebooks

Moleskine, known primarily for those little hardcover notebooks with an elastic strap, is a brand of many stories. The most recent one is of extraordinary brand success, leading in sixteen years from a single unassuming product to an IPO that netted over $600 million. Roots have been instrumental in the brand's rise from obscure cult item to today's badge of the creative class.

In Paris in the late 19th and early 20th centuries, small hand-made leather notebooks closed with a ribbon tie were a popular item in stationery stores. Expatriate artists and writers like van Gogh, Picasso, and Hemingway favored these notebooks, produced by local bookbinders. Later artists like English novelist/ travel writer Bruce Chatwin grew fiercely loyal to them. By the 1980s, they were getting harder to find. In his 1986 book *The Songlines*, Chatwin lamented that his beloved "moleskine" note-books (his name for them) had gone out of production.

In 1995 Maria Sebregondi, an Italian, read Chatwin's book and started to research the notebooks. She approached Modo & Modo, a small stationer in Milan, with the idea of producing them, and the company trademarked the name Moleskine in 1997. Sold as "The Legendary Notebook of Hemingway, Picasso and Chatwin," Moleskine developed a cult following, selling primarily through book and design stores, and enjoyed dramatic growth when distribution expanded throughout Europe and the U.S. in 1999.

In the early 2000s, Moleskine notebooks caught the attention of citizen-bloggers who created fan sites to publicize their love of the little notebooks. *Moleskinerie*, one of the most popular, was started by commercial photographer Armand Frasco in 2004. Within a few weeks he had 5,000 visitors/day. Volunteer marketers spurred growth to the point where Modo & Modo couldn't keep up with demand, and it sold the company to an investment group in 2006.

Artists and writers across the globe have seized upon the notebooks as a perfect vehicle for creative expression. The Moleskine brand has nurtured this connection through activities such as the Detour, a series of travelling exhibits/events held in cultural capitals that showcase notebooks from a wide range of creative luminaries.

But Moleskine sells about 10 million notebooks a year, a number far surpassing the needs of professional artists and writers. Today, the notebooks serve as an emblem of creative temperament and aspirations to a much wider audience. In our digitized, high-tech world they are a flourishing symbol of high-touch, with high quality production, creamy acid-free paper, and their signature elastic band. Though we may buy them at Target or Staples, we want to feel kinship with the avant-garde artists of fin-de-siècle Paris—or with contemporary indie creatives. And each little Moleskine we buy carries a copy of the brand's creation story.

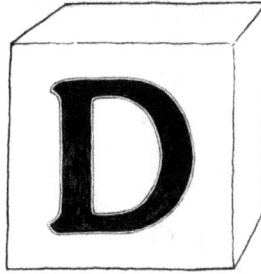

GETTING STARTED
WITH DEPTH

Essence

The 5 Whys method has been used as a tool for analyzing the root causes of a technical problem since Toyota pioneered the technique as part of its famed manufacturing process. As the name suggests, it simply means asking the question "Why?" consecutively five times to get at deeper and deeper issues.

We can adapt it to our purposes by modifying the question to explore areas of potential meaning.

- Why does your brand/product/service matter?

- Ask this question iteratively five times in a row and see what answers you get.

- Don't do this in a collective brainstorming session, where politics can constrain and shape responses.

- Instead, ask a range of people on your team and in your

company to come up with their own answers—and submit them anonymously.

Multidimensionality

Fans of the acclaimed HBO series "The Wire" will never forget Omar Little, the stick-up artist with the deep facial scar who regularly holds up drug dealers by outsmarting them. We remember him because of his layers, contradictions, and intriguing details: Violent, but with a strict moral code. Gay. Hates profanity. And he has strong brand preferences! He loves Newport cigarettes and Honey Nut Cheerios. The list goes on. Fascinating and endearing in his complexity, he reveals new dimensions as the series unfolds. Who would have guessed he loved mythology in middle school?

Take twenty to thirty minutes and think about at least three contemporary characters that intrigue you on TV, in books, or movies.

- Jot down what about them piques your interest. Pay particular attention to any beguiling contradictions.

- Now, think about how your company might view them. What's different? How do you feel about the difference? Is anything important missing that might be relevant to your brand or another brand?

- If your company works with personas, try rewriting one or two personas by working in a few contradictions based on the above exercise.

Roots

Exploring Roots is a fascinating endeavor, one that can potentially lead in many fruitful directions. Here are two areas to get you started.

Origins

How did your brand come to be? Who created it? How—and why? Your goal here is to develop a rich and compelling creation story. This may well overlap in certain areas with a probe for Essence.

- If a story already exists, can you add to it through additional research? If the existing story is fairly dry, is there an authentic way to make it more engaging by bringing in a more human dimension? Impact of the brand/company on customers, on the community, even the founder and his/her family are potential directions to consider.

- How does the creation story align with the brand today? Are there places where the brand went off-track? If so, what were the consequences?

- It's possible that your brand may have no meaningful origins. Many brands, for example, have simply been developed as copycats, piggybacking on something original created elsewhere. In this case, can you explore the origins of the company itself and connect how this ties with the brand?

Archetypal possibilities

Some brands seem to have a natural cohesiveness to them—a

subliminal storyline we recognize at some level. Consider the following, and how they seem to make intuitive sense:

- Harley-Davidson as Outlaw

- Starbucks as Explorer

- Johnson & Johnson as Caregiver

These brands embody classic archetypes, whether consciously or not. Archetypes are universal narratives (the Mother, the Warrior, the Lover, etc.) that contain a host of recognizable associations. They add instant Depth and help cut through clutter by leveraging things we already know and value.

- Together with your marketing team, read *The Hero and the Outlaw: Building Extraordinary Brands Through the Power of Archetypes*[7] by Margaret Mark and Carol S. Pearson. Although slightly dated, this book is an excellent introduction to archetypes in a brand and marketing context.

"The least of a thing with a meaning is worth more in life than the greatest of things without it."
–ANONYMOUS

E

IS FOR EMOTION

"

People don't ask for facts when they're making up
their minds. They would rather have one good
soul-satisfying emotion than a dozen facts.

ROBERT KEITH LEAVITT
Voyages and Discoveries

WHAT GREAT BRANDS KNOW

EMOTION

Nearly every aspect of right-brain marketing has the potential for emotional impact. Whether it's Beauty or Equanimity, or connecting with Roots, we are evoking Emotion in some way. And that's the whole point: we want to make customers care, and caring involves Emotion.

If/when companies contemplate Emotion, their first thoughts run to creating an emotional bond between customers and their brand. These thoughts are almost always linear and self-centered. What can I do/say/show about *me me me* to make people *buy buy buy*? This kind of Emotion-thinking is sanctioned in business, so marketers are allowed to throw money at it: hire the agency, make that cool ad. These kinds of efforts can be effective. But they are only a small part of the story.

First of all, whatever bond customers feel isn't really about you, the brand. It's about us. How you make us feel about ourselves. And you only have so much control over that.

Once you get past this safe, sanctioned area of brand ego, dealing with Emotion gets trickier, for more reasons than you might imagine. Some skepticism is hard to argue with. In a world that demands objective data and reliable measures, how on earth do you "do Emotion"? It's hard to measure, much less predict or control. And measurement, prediction, and control are central to how most businesses are run.

Other challenges are deeper and, frankly, more treacherous. Emotion is messy, imprecise, and deeply personal — the opposite of what the left brain understands and values. And in the data-driven business world, left-brainers are increasingly in charge. Let's be honest: few analytical superstars are good at the warm fuzzies, or even comfortable with them. Emotion can be deeply unsettling to the powerful and emotionally unskilled. So championing Emotion can be a perilous uphill battle, and that's without even hinting at the potential minefield of gender baggage.

Yet Emotion has huge potential to ignite and sustain success. Staying open to the emotional impact you're having on customers, whether intentional or not, is vital to avoiding potential disasters. Understanding customers' feelings and perspectives can lead to major innovations. Engaging with them directly and personally on an emotional level can win customers for life. Besides, Emotion isn't just reserved for customers. Your business can benefit enormously from bringing it into your dealings with employees.

Three main aspects of Emotion we'll discuss are Attunement, Empathy, and Engagement.

> **"The exaltation of reason over feeling leads
> to a society of reasonable duds."**
> **−RICK JAROW**

ATTUNEMENT

Being receptive and aware

Attunement is the starting point for any work with Emotion. Few companies will fully embrace Emotion and intentionally choose to engage with their customers (or employees) on that basis. Yet they still have an emotional impact—and they need to be aware of it.

WHAT ATTUNEMENT IS: Attunement is careful listening for emotional content. It means being open to and aware of the impact you're having, even (and especially) when you may not like what you hear.

WHAT ATTUNEMENT IS NOT: Attunement is not taking customer satisfaction surveys and analyzing the results. While such research can be helpful, even critical, it's only part of the story.

Even the best research can't prevent destructive, boneheaded decisions.

WHY ATTUNEMENT MATTERS: Ignoring your emotional impact creates huge blind spots that can be devastating—even fatal—to your brand or business, especially in today's hyper-connected social media world. By contrast, active Attunement, especially listening respectfully to those whom you displease or disappoint, can lead to important course corrections, opportunities, and breakthroughs.

Unfortunately, Attunement rarely gets the top-level attention it deserves. For one thing, bad news is seldom embraced gladly, especially at the top. Corporate culture often rewards party-line playback over candor and unwelcome reality checks.

Failure of Attunement is most dangerous when your customer's freedom of choice is illusory. Many large, profitable companies simply don't get this. Their world *feels* competitive to them, their rivals *feel* as real as those in any other category. So they make the mistake of thinking that their success is earned and their customers are there by choice. On the ground, though, genuine choice may not really exist—or it may be really, really inconvenient to leave.

In theory, we *can* change our bank, wireless provider, Internet service, etc. In practice, it can be a royal pain in the butt. So, like many a bad marriage or relationship, we stay just because the switching costs are too high. But we notice every time we're slighted or taken for granted—and we seethe.

No matter how big a brand may be, it's ultimately doomed if a large chunk of its customer base hangs by a thread, primed for that last straw. Remember AOL? Who's next: Verizon? Microsoft?

"When people talk, listen completely.
Most people never listen."
–ERNEST HEMINGWAY

TD Bank

We've all had it up to our eyeballs with big banks that don't listen. Customers of the Big Four (Bank of America, Citigroup, J.P. Morgan Chase, and Wells Fargo) can readily cite examples of indifference or even mistreatment by their bank. Bank of America's infamous but short-lived plan in 2011 to charge customers $5/month to use their debit cards still reverberates today. But in an industry famous for ignoring its customers, one bank is actually a model of Attunement.

The Toronto-Dominion Bank isn't often in the limelight. It has a sterling credit ranking (AAA ranking by Moody's) and a solid reputation, placing 12th among 30 banks in *American Banker*'s most recent survey of bank reputation. (The Big Four dominated the bottom quintile). In Toronto, it's also known for changing the city skyline with its headquarters, designed by Mies van der Rohe. Overall, it's pretty low-key.

Yet it has its own distinction: in a notoriously impersonal industry, TD Bank actively speaks about Emotion. In particular, it talks a lot about "Wow," which it defines as "the company's emotional attachment to customers and employees." While it goes about its everyday banking business, it also tries to create Wow! Moments for customers. Its recent TV campaign contrasts big-bank indifference to customers with its own attention to small moments, from conveniences like free coin-counting to an umbrella escort to your car when it rains. Signs encouraging employees to "Wow! the Customer with Every Contact" are common in training.

TD Bank also recognizes that banking is too often all about "no." Banks are quick to deny requests and hide behind arcane rules, leaving customers feeling unheard and dismissed preemptively. Instead, TD tries hard to say "yes" in primary dealings with customers. According to Fred Reichheld of Bain & Company, TD Bank "trains customer-facing employees to satisfy any client requests that don't violate the bank's policies and reinforces this with a '1 to say Yes, 2 to say No' rule. The goal is to find a way to say 'yes,' even if it requires a creative solution. When employees can't say 'yes' without breaking the rules, they must seek guidance from a supervisor. They can't simply say 'no' and move on to the next customer."[1]

They also invest a lot to measure how they're doing. TD has avidly embraced the Net Promoter Score (NPS), a metric pioneered by Reichheld, which sorts customers into promoters, passives, and detractors based on their response to a single question (how likely would they be to recommend the brand/company?). The bar to qualify as a promoter (answering 9 or 10 on a 0 to 10-point scale) is fairly high. And frankly, most banks don't fare too well on the NPS. According to a 2011 *Forbes* article, the average NPS score for U.S. banks was 13%, though for a national bank with branches (like Bank of America) the score was actually negative (-6%), with detractors outnumbering promoters[2]. In Bain's 2012 NPS survey of banks, TD Bank scored a 31 in the U.S. (Northeast) and was the top loyalty leader among national banks in Canada at 29 — not stratospheric, but solid.[3]

TD Bank has renamed NPS the Customer Wow! Index. Every day it calls 9,000 customers to gauge their satisfaction. When TD callers reach a detractor (someone who's given them 0-6 on a 0-10 scale), they ask permission to have a local bank employee contact the customer to try to make the situation right.

Which bank would you prefer: one indifferent to its emotional impact on customers or one actively pursuing Attunement?

EMPATHY

Understanding the feelings of others

"Are you safe? Are you in a warm place?" If you get into an accident, these are the questions you'll hear when Zipcar answers your call. Not "What is your Zipcar number?"

We have become so inured to impersonal treatment that we are left slack-jawed when a company acknowledges our emotional reality as important. Not via the canned "I'm-sorry-you've-experienced-difficulties" script of the traditional customer service line, but a with a vibrant human connection.

WHAT EMPATHY IS: Empathy is the capacity to understand other people's feelings and to see the world from their perspective. It means acknowledging the emotional reality of the people with whom you're engaging and meeting them at that place.

WHAT EMPATHY IS NOT: Empathy is not ersatz sympathy, a breezy "I feel your pain" angle used as simply another tool to sell them your product or service.

WHY EMPATHY MATTERS: Empathy *may be the single most important source of true innovation* — ahead of technology. While much new technology is remarkable, plenty of it is simply whiz-bang stuff that can be done by talented engineers. (Whether it should be done or makes a lasting positive impact are different questions.) Empathy, however, creates powerful new products and services with staying power because it starts with people: their behavior, needs, and yearnings. Two quick examples:

Over twenty years ago, Huggies introduced Pull-Ups Training Pants for toddlers. Pampers, the leading diaper brand, had considered the idea — and dismissed it as too small. But Huggies saw the opportunity differently, through an empathic lens. By acknowledging parents' desire to empower their growing children's sense of self ("I'm a big kid now!"), it became the top brand and left its rival in the dust for years.

Until recently, if you had juvenile diabetes, your choices were pretty grim: giving yourself lots of shots every day or wearing a pump on your belt. Most kids opted for shots, because they could be done privately. A pump shouted: I'm different. Working with Insulet, design firm Continuum developed the OmniPod, a tiny, disposable pump with a 3-day insulin supply regulated by a wireless handheld controller. In a few short years, OmniPod has become a $1 billion business, in large part because it allows users to maintain privacy about their disease.

Empathy is not just for new products, however. Offering real empathy whenever we engage with customers is hugely powerful. When our feelings are seen to matter, we feel seen. We matter as people: not just wallets, accounts, or transactions. This experience—scandalously rare as it is—touches us deeply and creates a bond few competitors can break.

"If there is any one secret of success, it lies in the ability to get the other person's point of view and see things from his angle as well as your own."
—HENRY FORD

Bridgeport Financial

Deadbeat. The synonyms aren't pretty. They include words like loafer, good-for-nothing, sponger, and harsher terms like parasite, barnacle, and leech.

People behind on their payments are treated as deadbeats by the collections industry. In a book brimming with remarkable stories, *Start with Why: How Great Leaders Inspire Everyone to Take Action*, Simon Sinek shares the tale of Christine Harbridge, who started working for a collections agency in Sacramento while still in college.

> *"Harbridge was immediately taken by the harshness of the tone that all the collectors used with those from whom they aimed to collect unpaid debts. 'They would hound them, and practically threaten them,' she said. 'They would do anything it took to get information from them.'"*[4]

With bonuses hinging on how much money they collected, debt collectors strove to maximize what they got from every individual or business they called that was behind on payments. According to Harbridge, her boss and colleagues, "all kind, gracious people," were transformed in the course of their work: "when they were on the phone to collect a debt, these same people turned passive-aggressive, rude and often mean."[5] When she found herself doing the same thing, she vowed to find a better way.

Harbridge started her own collections firm in San Francisco, Bridgeport Financial, based on a radical premise for the industry:

"everyone has a story and deserves to be listened to." Believing "that agents would have more success treating people with respect than badgering them,"[6] she had her employees focus on establishing rapport with the debtor and getting the truth from them about their situation. In an industry characterized by mean, she emphasized nice. Bonuses were based on how many thank-you notes agents sent (after substantive conversations with debtors). Get-well cards were sent to debtors who were sick.

And the results? Bridgeport Financial ended up collecting three times the industry average. Moreover, according to Sinek: "most of the people and companies who were initially being pursued ended up doing more business with the original company that sent the collections agency after them in the first place. This is almost unprecedented in the collections industry."[7] A 2003 article in the *San Francisco Business Times* noted that Harbridge's firm was able to recover 100 percent of the debt for some clients, a success rate that helped spur revenue growth from $540,000 in 2000 to $1 million in 2002.[8] She sold the firm in 2006 for an undisclosed sum.

Through Empathy, Harbridge was able to accomplish several things: providing her agents a work environment aligned with their better natures, offering debtors respect and compassion, and creating a highly successful business in the process.

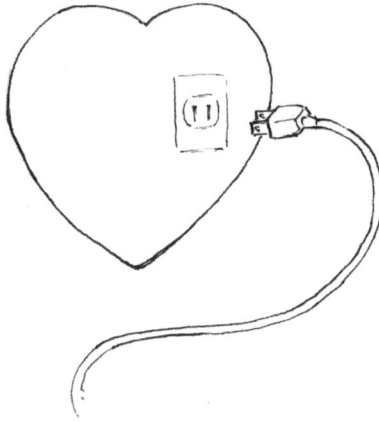

ENGAGEMENT

Forming a meaningful connection

Contemplating a customer pain point is a widespread instance of a brand or business dealing in the realm of Emotion. Emotion also shows up when using Empathy to uncover other opportunities. Most brands use these insights to do something finite—launch a new product, tweak an ad, refresh the call center script—then walk away. Job done! Problem solved! Opportunity seized!

But Emotion isn't a one-time thing solved by a single insight or action. Truly remarkable brands understand this and see ongoing emotional Engagement as a source of extraordinary value—and benefits—on many levels.

No standardized "Emotion" nomenclature exists in business, so I want to differentiate between cultivating an emotional attachment to your brand and what I'm calling Engagement.

Whether you call it attachment, fondness, affection, or whatever, companies want customers to like, even love their brands, for good reason. Positive emotional connection helps create preference and loyalty, insulates against competition, allows for premium pricing, and more.

Companies work to create emotional attachment to their brands in many ways, but the chief route is:

Create a distinctive and compelling offering

Communicate how/why it's great

Get people to buy it

Rinse and repeat b) and c)

Once we've understood our customers' perspective and how we can get through to them, we've got what we need.

WHAT ENGAGEMENT IS: Engagement means engaging directly with customers' emotions, touching their hearts through authentic person-to-person interactions over time. It starts with Empathy, but it doesn't stop there. It's ongoing and generally deeper.

WHAT ENGAGEMENT IS NOT: Engagement is not just structuring cheerful customer interactions. Creating pleasant experiences is valuable, but real Engagement involves a wider emotional range and may well happen off-script, in a place of shared humanity. It's also experienced more individually and more deeply than generalized "brand love."

WHY ENGAGEMENT MATTERS: Engagement offers companies everything from an early warning system for problems to an opportunity to create evangelists.

Much that's been written about the deep bonds people have with the brands in their lives is massively overblown. In most cases, we'd be perfectly fine if you disappeared tomorrow, though we might be sorry you're gone. With true Engagement, we'd feel a genuine, recurring sense of loss. And it would be a specific you-shaped loss, not just regret over the passing of an era.

My Starbucks survey asks if the barista knows my name (and they all do). My TJ's cashier tells me about a great meal he made with two of the ingredients in my basket. On a transactional level, I've bought their coffee and groceries. On a human level, they've created places I like to go, people I like to see. Their competitors don't have a chance at my business.

"What your heart thinks is great, is great.
The soul's response is always right."

−RALPH WALDO EMERSON

Zappos

By now, most readers have probably heard that Zappos is an innovative company with legendary service. Online competitors have copied its innovations, like free shipping both ways. And other retailers, like Nordstrom, also offer fabled customer service. But Zappos has a secret ingredient we don't often talk about: emotional Engagement, which is central to the company's remarkable culture.

According to CEO Tony Hsieh "every call is perceived as a way to make a positive emotional connection with a customer."[9] On a call, Customer Loyalty Team (CLT) agents (as call center employees are known) might ask about the dog barking in the background or send flowers to a bride, says Jane Judd, senior manager of the CLT. While Nordstrom has attentive service and generous return policies, there's a formality to the friendliness: they don't often engage with you personally and emotionally.

Zappos encourages its employees to use their judgment and personality when connecting with customers. There are no scripts, nor are there specific policies to handle each customer situation. This makes interactions more real, allowing opportunities for creativity, spontaneity, and compassion. An *Inc.* magazine article recounts a story told by Hsieh about a woman who had ordered boots for her husband, but he died in a car accident after she placed the order:

> *"The day after she called to ask for help with the return, she received a flower delivery. The call center rep had ordered the*

flowers without checking with a supervisor and billed them to the company. 'At the funeral, the widow told her friends and family about the experience,' Hsieh said, his voice cracking and his eyes tearing up ever so slightly. 'Not only was she a customer for life, but so were those 30 or 40 people at the funeral.'"[10]

The Zappos call center is a busy place. On average, it fields 5,000 calls a day and 1,200 e-mails/week—and more during the holiday season. Though time per call is a standard metric elsewhere, Zappos doesn't use it. There are no limits on call time. Instead the company looks at the total percentage of time CLT agents spend on the phone. According to Derek Carder, customer loyalty operations manager for the Zappos, "It's more important that we make an emotional connection with the customer, rather than just quickly getting them off the phone."[11] The longest recorded call is eight hours.

Zappos' customers are fiercely loyal, accounting for roughly 75% of company sales. The company spends almost nothing on advertising. Instead, its customers spread the word.

The company's goal, according to Hsieh, is to "deliver happiness in a box. Our customers call and e-mail us to say that's how it feels when a Zappos box arrives. And that's how we view this company."[12]

GETTING STARTED
WITH EMOTION

Attunement

Attunement should be used upfront to guide decision-making and avoid costly mistakes. It's also essential when mopping up after a mess. Here are some ways to embrace Attunement.

Learn from the great disasters

Within recent memory, two massive failures in Attunement are worth studying in detail:

• When Netflix announced its decision to split into two separate companies (streaming vs. DVD rentals) in mid-2011, its clumsy efforts cost $12 billion in market capitalization in a few months.

• Bank of America's disastrous effort in September 2011 to charge a $5/month fee for using debit cards was retracted in five weeks after public outcry. The impact continues to reverberate.

Research and review these two case studies, then discuss the following questions with your team:

- What emotional issues were ignored when the companies made the initial decision? And the announcement?

- What assumptions did the companies make that proved to be faulty?

- Did the company add insult to injury in their response to public reaction? If so, how/why? What could/should have been done differently?

- What should each company do to prevent such a mistake in the future?

Establish a kitchen council

Businesses understandably focus on the financial and logistical impact of decisions they make, but they often fail to fully consider the potential human and emotional impact on their customers. Decision makers, who live and breathe the internal perspective, can get very isolated from reality on the ground.

You need a warning system for averting potential disasters. While your company/brand should have ongoing mechanisms to get customer insight proactively, at the very least you can establish an informal panel of intelligent, articulate, emotionally-grounded people outside the company who can be consulted for open, unfiltered, confidential feedback on potential decisions. Scanning social media for trouble signs—and having the right people within the company empowered to address potential issues as they arise—can be an important step here.

Empathy

Here are two starting points for getting acquainted with Empathy and integrating it into your brand/business:

Read a book

An excellent book on Empathy in a business context is *Wired to Care: How Companies Prosper When They Create Widespread Empathy*, by Dev Patnaik[13]. The author, who teaches innovation at Stanford and founded Jump Associates (a Bay-area strategy/design firm) maintains "that the problem with business today isn't a lack of innovation; it's a lack of empathy." His book draws on compelling stories of companies that have succeeded by looking at the world through their customers' eyes—and those who've stumbled because they haven't. Great examples, and a fun and interesting read.

Enlist design expertise

Empathy for the user lies at the heart of design. Practitioners in the field start with behavioral observation to understand the context in which people experience (or might experience) your product or service.

- If your firm can afford a design strategy firm, hire one to work with you as you develop a new product/service you are considering or improving an existing offering.

- If a design firm is beyond your means, consider scoping out a project for a student team. Design strategy (think IDEO) is a hot field, and graduate programs are springing up everywhere.

- At the very least, take a long, critical look at how you treat first-time customers at every point of contact. What happens when someone calls your help line? Or tries to get a question answered on your website? What frustrations have you experienced in your own lives with a new product or service—and how does that relate to how you treat your own customers?

Engagement

No company should attempt Engagement until it has essentially mastered Attunement and Empathy. A brand/business must earn the right to engage more deeply with customers—by being worthy of that level of interaction and trust.

If you feel you're at that point, terrific! Now, start small. Take a look at what you track, measure, and reward. This is often done on autopilot or by using industry standards, which may favor what's easy to measure and deemed "efficient." Reread the Brand Spotlights on Empathy (Bridgeport Financial) and Engagement (Zappos). Both companies take a deliberately different path towards measurement and incentives.

> "The goals of management are usually described in words like 'efficiency,' advantage,' 'value,' 'superiority,' 'focus,' and 'differentiation.' Important as these objectives are, they lack the power to rouse human hearts."
>
> —GARY HAMEL, *The Future of Management*

F

IS FOR FUN

66

A good and wholesome thing is a little harmless fun in this world; it tones a body up and keeps him human and prevents him from souring.

MARK TWAIN

FUN

It seems fitting that we should end with a principle that seems, on the surface, so lightweight—even frothy. After all, those folk in the annual reports and boardrooms sure seem to be doing solemn stuff, making the economy hum. Business is a serious undertaking, is it not?

Yes, but…

Customers and employees (even vendors!) are people. We can be fully committed to a profitable, efficient business and still be real people. Competence and effectiveness are musts, of course. But when lightness is also present, we connect in a more fully human way, and we're better able to bring out the best in one another. Far from being trivial, Fun provides important opportunities for creativity and connection.

The elements of Fun share common roots. Chief among them is a broadminded, large-hearted view of people, especially employees. Fun also includes a willingness to consider creative and non-linear paths to meeting company goals. The three dimensions of Fun are Joviality, Enjoyment, and Play. These Fundamentals are key to building the ultimate brand asset: the ability to deliver customer delight.

> **"People rarely succeed unless they are having fun in what they are doing."**
>
> −DALE CARNEGIE

JOVIALITY

Cheerfulness and good humor

The default in business is Bland. We may try to lighten things with a funny ad campaign now and then, but if you pick up the phone and call us, read our package, or visit our establishment, chances are you'll get Bland. Or should I say…businesslike?

Businesslike: *carrying out tasks efficiently without wasting time or being distracted by personal or other concerns; systematic and practical. – New Oxford American Dictionary*

Wow. Is it any wonder that cheerfulness and humor seem out of place? In a world where the very adjective to describe business equates with orderly, impersonal, no-nonsense activity, anything extraneous seems, at best, unprofessional.

This is a real shame, because Joviality offers real power. It can forge strong connections and provide a winning edge—not to mention make the workday more enjoyable.

WHAT JOVIALITY IS: Joviality is bringing genuine cheerfulness and levity into how you engage with your customers. It means finding opportunities for natural ease and merriment. While the "business" at hand is done effectively and professionally, it's not overlaid with excessive solemnity simply because that's been part of traditional business culture.

WHAT JOVIALITY IS NOT: Joviality is not the gratuitous yucks of an ad campaign. Humorous ad campaigns tend to come in two flavors (sometimes swirled together):

AnyBrand entertainment: This has a comical storyline that's generic (it could work for nearly any brand) and mostly superfluous—there for entertainment value vs. real communication.

Competitor-bashing snark: In this version, the brand hero puts competitors down gleefully with withering sarcasm. There's lots of brand ego (see! look how great and cool I am!) and an underlying nastiness.

Brands with Joviality may have humorous ads, but the tone is different. There's less ego and more above-the-fray drollness that invites connection. The tone: "Isn't this a crazy world? It doesn't have to be this way."

Why Joviality matters: Joviality creates a warm and friendly space—a refuge from both the general impersonality of business and from the sense of grasping and scarcity we often feel (Look at me! Buy me, now! My competitor sucks!). Instead, there's a sunny feeling, a tiny burst of playfulness and abundance in the moment.

Certainly humor is a key ingredient of Joviality, but it's not the only one. There is a quality of lightness, of not taking things too seriously. And there's a keen sense of trust: faith in the quality of the product or service being offered, trust in employees without excessive scripting and control, and faith in the customer to make a wise decision.

Authentic Joviality says: "Yes, we're here to buy and sell, but we can all be people, too." It offers a playful touch of shared humanity, and it produces smiles that last.

"Laughter is the sun that drives winter
from the human face."

−VICTOR HUGO

Southwest Airlines

BusinessWeek columnist and blogger Steve McKee wrote in 2011 about his experience on a recent flight. The flight attendant had the cabin in stitches on takeoff and landing as he delivered safety and landing briefings with the flair of a stand-up comedian. McKee reflected how he's "come to expect that type of lighthearted humor from Southwest Airlines" and appreciates "their attempts to make traveling just a little less of a hassle."[1]

Only while taxiing to his arrival gate did he realize he'd just flown on American Airlines.

Southwest Airlines has become so identified with inflight humor that any levity in the skies immediately brings Southwest to mind. That's the sign of a powerful brand. Founded in 1971 to provide service within Texas, Southwest was best known in its early days for long-legged stewardesses in hot pants and go-go boots. Today, it's a living embodiment of Joviality, where cheerfulness and playful humor prevail in an industry mostly characterized by earnest corporate pomposity.

Southwest flight attendants are famous for onboard pranks and jokes. Passengers on the terminal-facing side of a plane have been asked to press their faces against the window, "to show their competitor what a full flight looks like." Flight personnel have hidden in overhead luggage compartments to surprise unwary boarders, and in-flight contests have awarded prizes for socks with holes.

Levity is not reserved for the in-flight experience alone. In 1992, legendary Southwest CEO and co-founder Herb Kelleher resolved a potential trademark dispute with Stevens Aviation (over similar ad slogans) by an arm wrestling match. Promotional videos for the charity event, "Malice in Dallas," showed him "training" while chain-smoking and weight-lifting giant bottles of Wild Turkey whiskey.[2] To combat high-stress jobs, employees at corporate HQ have been allowed to wear pajamas for a day.

Joviality is only part of Southwest's famed corporate culture. Their people-focused approach defies conventionality by explicitly putting employees first, in their "magic formula:"

Happy Employees=Happy Customers=Increased Business/ Profits=Happy Shareholders![3]

It's a formula that has been working extremely well. Southwest has become the largest low-cost carrier in the United States, serving more passengers domestically than any other airline. Among other distinctions, Southwest:

• Has the fewest customer complaints (2013 Airline Quality Rating report).

• Was ranked first by *Consumer Reports* in 2011.

• Has enjoyed 40 consecutive years of profitability.

• Is among the top 10 most admired companies in the world (*Forbes* 2013).

ENJOYMENT

Creating pleasurable experiences

Wasn't that nice?

How often do you feel that way after you've just used a product, visited a business establishment, or interacted with a company employee (in person, online, by phone)? Not nearly often enough. When it happens, it's notable—and it wins us over.

WHAT ENJOYMENT IS: Enjoyment means creating conditions for an enjoyable experience—one we can recognize and appreciate as pleasant whether the experience is core to the primary business purpose or not.

While it's easier to achieve with a brand that's inherently experiential (like a retailer, restaurant, or other service business), some products are also capable of generating Enjoyment.

WHAT ENJOYMENT IS NOT: Enjoyment is not a scenario specifically orchestrated to deliver "fun." You don't have to be a Disney to deliver Enjoyment. In fact, the engineered experience of a Disney theme park feels tightly wound, its massive underlying control system nearly palpable.

Enjoyment doesn't have to be a big deal—or to be reserved for leisure-time activities. Instead, it simply means envisioning a pleasurable, relevant context for the product or service at hand and working to deliver it.

WHY ENJOYMENT MATTERS: Enjoyment makes us happy. It makes us want to do business with you again and to tell others about you. With true Enjoyment, we experience a sense of ease from the enterprise itself that contributes to our own pleasure. You have created something delightful not just to sell us something, but because the world is a better place when there is more to enjoy. Enjoyment lifts our spirits and gives us a feeling of expansiveness. It puts us on your team, the yay-world!, yay-journey (vs. destination) team.

"I adore simple pleasures.
They are the last refuge of the complex."
—OSCAR WILDE

Bespoke Innovations

Products are usually designed to solve a problem, create an agreeable experience for the user, or both. Seldom does their impact go much further. It's hard to imagine a product that also creates pleasant experiences for complete strangers. Here's an example to ponder.

Imagine a prosthetic leg that creates confidence for the wearer—and invites conversation and admiration from strangers.

Losing a leg is an undeniably traumatic experience. Fortunately, advances in biomedical engineering allow today's amputees to reclaim mobility unheard of even a few years ago. Yet there is more to a leg than functionality. Among other things, the amputee faces a deep loss of identity. Even subtle issues like the way a trouser leg hangs can be a daily reminder of loss. He/she also faces a recurring interpersonal challenge: awkwardness in social situations when the prosthesis is exposed.

Bespoke Innovations addresses these "softer" challenges. Founded in 2009 by an industrial designer and an orthopedic surgeon (and acquired in 2012 by 3D Systems Corporation), Bespoke developed Fairings, modular additions to prosthetic legs that allow for customization by contour—and personality. In addition to providing a customized shape, Bespoke offers options for materials and styling, allowing wearers to make a fashion statement and express their creativity.

"I've just got to tell you that's the coolest leg ever,"[4] said a TSA airport security agent to one woman, Deborah, an amputee who has taken to wearing skirts to show off her custom legs. Deborah's wardrobe of Fairings includes one in black lace and chrome, one wrapped with tattooed leather, one suggesting fishnet stockings, and another appearing as white lace. She notes that her Fairings allow her a greater sense of confidence, identity and self-expression.

Instead of awkwardness and silence, averted eyes or gawking, the experience is transformed. The Fairing says something unique and positive about the wearer, who becomes not only a real person in others' eyes, but an interesting one. Uncomfortable feelings are replaced by curiosity, even admiration.

Chad Crittenden, an amputee athlete (and competitor in Season 9 of "Survivor") describes his Fairing as a "conversation piece" that allows him to represent people with disabilities.[5]

Chances are after such a conversation, people will mention the encounter to others, triggering a ripple effect of positive feeling. Six degrees of Enjoyment. Wouldn't that be nice?

PLAY

Freedom or scope for action;
enjoyable activity

"That's why they call it work." Most of us have heard (or used) this phrase. It's work vs. fun. Work is what we're paid for when we show up at the office, and our dread of Monday is nearly universal.

Not everywhere, though. Some lucky dogs actually enjoy their work (imagine that!). A key way to transform work from drudgery to a pleasurable experience is to offer opportunities for autonomy. When you have more say in what you do, it's vastly more enjoyable.

For example, most jobs at the Ritz-Carlton are far from glamorous, but the company does offer something exceptional: respect and trust. Every employee is authorized to spend up to $2,000 on a guest—without approval from his/her general manager—to create a wonderful guest experience. Staff members are able to use their creativity, initiative, and people skills, which may not otherwise be tapped on a regular basis in their jobs.

WHAT PLAY IS: Play is mostly thought of as recreational activity with no practical purpose. Here we mean Play as freedom and ease. Work that feels like Play. Our use of the word also invokes other meanings of Play, such as:

• Freedom of movement within a space, as part of a mechanism;

• Freedom for action or scope of activity.

WHAT PLAY IS NOT: Play is not goofiness on the job: Ping-pong in the break room, or a Halloween costume contest. While these kinds of stress-busting or team-building opportunities can offer a welcome pause, they're peripheral—and in some cases they serve largely as a badge of Coolness.

WHY PLAY MATTERS: Play helps grow both the top and bottom line.

Top line growth: Play fuels innovation. When freedom is present, good ideas have room to surface and thrive. The results can be anything from creating customer delight (and loyalty) at the Ritz-Carlton to developing breakthrough new products and services.

Some companies explicitly carve out Play time for employees: paid time for passion projects outside their regular work. This investment may yield nothing, but it's also given rise to huge successes. Google's legendary 20% time, for example, has led to Gmail, Google Earth, Google News, Google Talk, and AdSense.

Bottom line growth: Play helps attract and retain good people. When companies offer opportunities for self-direction, they tap intrinsic motivation, a much more powerful force than traditional carrot-and-stick incentives. In today's economy, the best employees are not yesterday's compliant cogs. They're skilled, resourceful, creative—and in demand. They're precisely the people most likely to thrive under autonomy and bolt from a tight leash.

"I never did a day's work in my life—it was all fun."
—THOMAS EDISON

3M

It all started with a massive failure. The plan was to mine corundum, valuable to makers of grinding wheels, but the mine contained only anorthosite, which was practically worthless. From this humbling start, 3M has grown to be one of the most innovative companies on earth.

3M's near-death experience led to a conscious push toward innovation and diversification. No more eggs-in-one-basket. In *Built to Last: Successful Habits of Visionary Companies*, Jim Collins and Jerry Porras describe how this approach led to the creation of a remarkable culture prizing individual initiative. Phrases "that would be chanted often by 3Mers throughout its history" include:

"Listen to anyone with an original idea, no matter how absurd it might sound at first."

"Encourage; don't nitpick. Let people run with an idea."

"Hire good people, and leave them alone."

"If you put fences around people, you get sheep. Give people the room they need."

"Encourage experimental doodling."

"Give it a try—and quick!"[6]

How many corporate denizens would say their own workplaces are this open to creativity, experimentation, and autonomy?

In 1948, as the rest of post-war America was getting back to work in increasingly large, rigid, and hierarchical organizations, 3M took an unusual step, establishing 15 Percent Time. This was paid time that scientists and technical people could spend on projects of their own choosing (and is now available to all employees). Expensive and risky, it has nonetheless resulted in a huge array of successful innovations. According to 3M, 15 Percent Time has led to: Scotch® Brand Tapes, Post-it® Notes, Scotchgard™ Fabric Protector, automobile window treatment films, multilayer optical films and silicon adhesive systems for transdermal drug delivery

This remarkable freedom illustrates one core aspect of Play. At 3M, 15 Percent Time works particularly well because there's another element: an atmosphere of creative competition—Play as sport, or at least Science Fair. A *Fast Company* article describes an annual event where 200 employees from all over the company present their 15 Percent Time projects in a mammoth poster-session exhibition. Wayne Maurer, an R&D manager in 3M's abrasives division, cites the event as an opportunity for people to showcase their "inner geek," noting: "For technical people, it's the most passionate and engaged event we have at 3M."[7]

Not everyone has the curiosity, drive, and interest to pursue new ideas. But in today's world, Innovate or Die is an ever more common imperative. Organizations need good ideas, and they need to attract and keep good people. Those willing to embrace Play are likely to be among the winners.

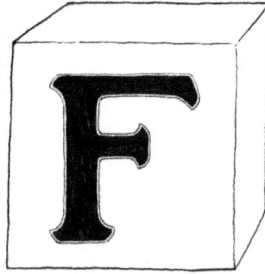

GETTING STARTED WITH FUN

The chief prerequisite for Fun may be outside the reach of many readers. Your organization must trust its employees, allow them freedom for initiative and see their personalities and imagination as powerful assets. It must also be willing to loosen up and not take itself so seriously. This is especially important in the areas of Joviality and Play.

If your organization has a "businesslike" culture, with little tolerance for anything that deviates from solemn efficiency, don't bother with Fun. Any efforts are likely to flop with customers and harden cynicism within your company. For reference, do the smiley face stickers they hand out at Walmart make shopping there fun, or do they just seem a little creepy? And what do you imagine Walmart employees might say about them when no manager is listening?

Joviality

Internal efforts

If you're not sure about your company's receptiveness to Joviality, consider the following:

April Fool's: What would an April Fool's issue of an in-house newsletter be about?

• What would the tone be? Who would write it, and how would it be received?

Gallows humor: It's hard to imagine an organization where gallows humor among employees doesn't exist. If private gallows humor were to be heard by others, how would it be received by management? By employees in other areas/departments?

External efforts

One essential element of Joviality is the humor must be good-natured. There is a little room for playful competitor-bashing if done in a friendly spirit, but there is no room for caustic humor or anything mean-spirited, done at someone's expense.

Enjoyment

Here are two questions to trigger ideas about bringing Enjoyment to your brand (focusing especially on services):

What?

What would Enjoyment look like? Here you may wish to contemplate the following aspects:

- **Universal:** Elements like friendly interchanges with employees, congenial surroundings, service with a sense of orderliness and fair-dealing, etc. would be welcome in any business.

- **Specific:** What fundamental needs/yearnings does your brand address?

Please note: this isn't the same as what problem you solve for customers. For example, both Trader Joe's and Wegman's (a grocery chain, fabled for its cult-like following) sell groceries, which addresses a fundamental need for food, convenience, etc. TJ's focuses on a yearning for adventure—on a budget, while Wegman's stresses sensory experience.

How?

How might you begin to incorporate elements of Enjoyment?

Here readers can benefit from having reached the end of the book. Congratulations! By now you have an ample trove of resources upon which to draw. As you revisit earlier sections of the book, here are some specific right-brain approaches that can contribute greatly to creating Enjoyment:

A is for Art:
- **Beauty:** Incorporating opportunities for aesthetic and sensory pleasure.

- **The Arts:** Introducing imaginative elements drawn from the realm of Art.

B is for Balance:

- **Harmony:** Aligning the components of your experience into a pleasing whole.

- **Equanimity:** Embracing a calm, non-commercial tonality.

D is for Depth:

- **Multidimensionality:** Viewing your customers in larger, more holistic ways to identify opportunities to delight.

- **Roots:** Anchoring your experience in authentically relevant domains outside the immediate brand/category sphere.

Play

Looking for suggestions on how to tap your employees' imagination and gather exciting new ideas? Look elsewhere. Ideas are not the starting point for Play. In fact, you're likely to hear groans (stifled or audible, depending on your organizational culture) when you announce another brainstorming or ideation session. Chances are, you have no shortage of ideas already. The scarce resources are time and opportunity to implement.

The starting point for Play is to understand the lived daily experience of your employees, and how this relates to the ideal conditions for creativity and productivity. For this, I heartily recommend the following.

Read a book

The Progress Principle: Using Small Wins to Ignite Joy, Engagement and Creativity at Work by Teresa Amabile and Steven Kramer.[8] Based on rigorous analysis of 12,000 diary entries from 238 employees at 7 companies, the authors, a Harvard Business School professor and her psychologist husband, ably demonstrate that broad, sweeping strategy is not the key to success. Instead it is small things that count: small but pivotal decisions and interactions by management that create conditions in which employees experience small wins. These seemingly minor experiences add up to a mighty whole, enabling employees to experience a satisfying—even joyful—inner work life.

"Always leave enough time in your life to do something that makes you happy, satisfied, even joyous. That has more of an effect on economic well-being than any other single factor."

—PAUL HAWKEN

THE WAY
FORWARD

"

There is a candle in your heart,
ready to be kindled.
There is a void in your soul,
ready to be filled.
You feel it, don't you?'

RUMI

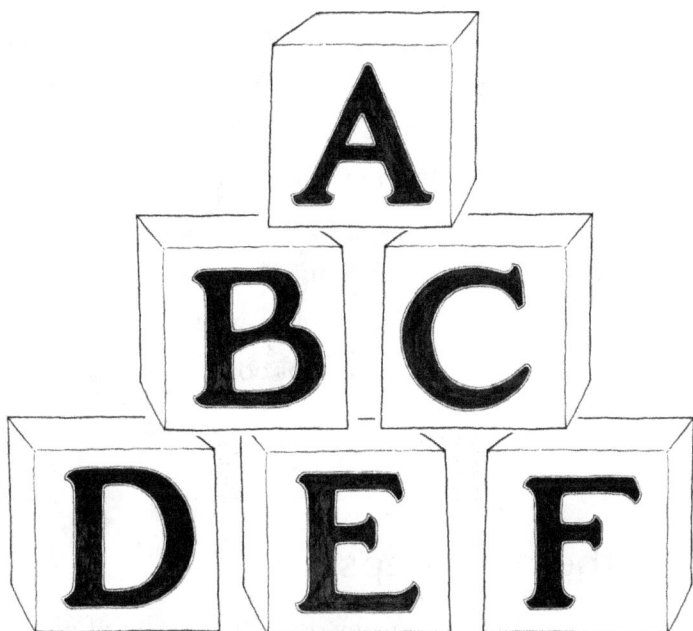

Your hero's journey

In the classic hero's journey, the tale begins in the everyday world when the hero receives a call to enter an unknown realm. Traveling through unfamiliar territory, he/she encounters marvels, perplexities, and challenges—and experiences an awakening.

If you picked up this book and have reached this point, you, too, experienced a call. You sensed that something was amiss in your familiar business and marketing world. You were willing to set off and explore new terrain. And on your journey you've encountered some strange and wondrous things: performance art to sample soap, a debt collection agency writing thank-you cards. Even a bank that listens!

Some of the ideas and examples you've encountered here may have resonated instantly, triggering a sense of excitement, perhaps even of homecoming. Others may seem confusing (or even irritating). Overall, though, I hope that your journey into right-brain land has prompted an awakening: a greater sense of what's possible—and what's missing. An understanding of how some brands have become Icons, and what next steps on that path might look like for your brand or company.

Now what?

Finding the next steps

The last part of the hero's journey doesn't get a lot of airtime. It's the return, the journey home. How do you bring your newfound knowledge back, and what do you do with it once you're there?

For those who run your own companies, this return journey is much easier. It can be an exciting and heady time as you sort through the possibilities for experimentation and change. For those who don't, however, this means returning to an organization that in all likelihood still wildly favors the left brain. How do you take your new understanding and integrate it into daily life back at the ranch?

The starting point is to find something everyone can agree on. One area of likely consensus is the nature of today's challenges. Few would dispute that markets are more cluttered and competitive, the pace of change swifter and more relentless, and customers more empowered and demanding than ever before.

These challenges demand robust, whole-brained solutions.

The next step is to seek opportunities for inclusive, both/and approaches. This book has focused primarily on making a case for the right brain in business and marketing, but it isn't a manifesto of right-brain supremacy. We need both kinds of thinking and expertise—and we need excellence in both.

Building a bridge toward a whole-brained approach

To build a case for whole-brained ways to address today's challenges, here is a brief summary of three common issues you might be facing in your business or role. We'll take a quick look at the upside and downsides of these lopsided perspectives and offer a few questions and examples, from the book and elsewhere, to help spark a more integrated approach.[1]

ISSUE #1

The left-brain focuses narrowly on what is already identified as important.

UPSIDE: Can offer opportunities for competitive advantage through greater depth of expertise.

DOWNSIDE: By discounting what it doesn't know or value, a brand/company risks:

- Limiting the range and quality of thinking and options considered.

- Making itself vulnerable to blindsiding.

- Promoting narrowly focused experts who prefer people like themselves, further constraining diversity of thought.

QUESTIONS/ISSUES FOR LB CONTEMPLATION:
- Do greater risks lie in incomplete mastery of what we're currently focused on—or in unexpected, disruptive possibilities we may not have considered?

- What's the balance of evidence in past industry shifts and fallen brand giants?

- Do greater opportunities for breakthroughs lie in further refinement and application of current thinking and existing processes—or in considering profoundly different ideas and approaches?

- What's our own record on sticking with the tried and true? What's happened to ideas that have felt uncomfortably new and different?

WHERE RB THINKING CAN HELP:
- Able to connect faint or distant dots of potential opportunity or danger. Adept at divergent thinking, which is essential to innovation. For example:

   o IKEA has become a hugely popular and beloved global brand by upending most everything in the furniture industry. Now extending beyond the domestic interior, it has developed flatpack refugee shelters and is poised to start selling solar panels in the U.K.

- A powerful resource for questioning assumptions and for asking "what if?" Consider:

  o The disastrous 1985 launch of "New Coke" to replace Coca-Cola might have been avoided if RB thinking had been allowed to question the primacy of blind taste tests.

ISSUE #2

The left brain excels at what is isolated and static.

UPSIDE: Develops deep mastery of discrete bodies of knowledge. Ideally suited to specialization.

DOWNSIDE: By overly focusing on the importance of specialized mastery, a brand/company often:

- Doesn't understand how the parts fit together or form a larger whole (and may not be especially interested).

- Is ill adapted to understanding complex issues that are interrelated and evolving.

QUESTIONS/ISSUES FOR LB CONTEMPLATION:
- Are the challenges you face on your brand/business discrete and isolated or intertwined?

- Are they evolving? Is the category in which you compete dynamic?

- Does your company rely regularly on standard tests and metrics, even when they may be outdated or irrelevant under changing circumstances?

- Do you require "deep expertise" even in areas that are new and fast-changing? Is it okay in your organization to not know something definitively?

WHERE RB THINKING CAN HELP:

- Skilled at discerning patterns and relationships. Good at seeing the whole and how the pieces fit together. For example:

  o Amazon, originally an online bookstore, has become the world's largest online retailer through a succession of shrewd moves into other categories, partnerships with other merchants, and innovations in everything from user experience to creating original products/services (e.g. Kindle) and content.

- Comfortable with uncertainty and change, which are viewed as inevitable. Forward-thinking and adept at seeing emerging issues and trends. Consider:

  o The graveyard of brands that were undisputed masters of a product, service or business model that proved obsolete knows no bounds. Recent brands like Blockbuster and Borders have joined earlier names like Polaroid, Digital Equipment Corporation and others extending back into time.

ISSUE #3

The left brain excels at what is abstract and lifeless. Offers linear, logical, sequential thinking.

UPSIDE:

- Helps create categories, methodologies, systems and models.

- Brings order and rationality to a world drowning in data.

- Good at manipulating numbers and abstractions.

DOWNSIDE: When a brand/company places disproportionate emphasis on abstractions, logic, and linear thinking, it is often:

- Unskilled at understanding people, especially in their complexity, variety and particularity.

- Poor at grasping the implications of what's experienced by real people in real contexts, including what numbers (however masterfully analyzed) may actually mean.

- Likely to favor coherence of its abstract system over a complex, multifaceted reality that may not fit its models.

- Ill-prepared to deal with anything requiring imagination, emotion, and holistic thinking.

- Prone to mechanistic perspectives and actions.

QUESTIONS/ISSUES FOR LB CONTEMPLATION:

- Increasing market fragmentation elevates the importance

of understanding ever-smaller niches. Can data mining alone identify where the opportunities are? Or could pairing analytical whizzes with others adept at insight into the real, everyday experience of people turbocharge your efforts?

- Social media offers new opportunities to connect with individuals and gives every consumer a megaphone. Given this new reality, how has your company addressed the need for skills in empathy and human understanding? Or is it primarily focused on tactics and metrics?

- In saturated, sophisticated markets, which is more likely to offer sustained advantage: discrete, functional benefit advances or a holistic approach that engages emotion and human aspirations?

WHERE RB THINKING CAN HELP:

- Good at providing imagination, empathy and insight into human beings and their real lives. For instance:

  o Trader Joe's founder Joe Coulombe saw emerging trends (more college degrees and international travel) and envisioned specific kinds of underserved customers (like teachers, engineers, public administrators).

- Skilled at understanding and using context, symbols, and emotional tonality. Consider:

  o Cirque du Soleil has built a global brand and loyal following by weaving Art, Depth and Emotion into a realm traditionally marked by a sequence of unrelated skill-based acts.

- Expert at discerning meaning and crafting narratives. For example:

  o Moleskine has built a profitable empire around a 19th century notebook replica by harnessing Depth, linking past traditions with contemporary creative aspirations. It has also embraced Art, successfully addressing a yearning for high-touch quality that has largely disappeared from our mass-market lives.

Revisiting the 2 x 2 matrix in the chapter How Great Brands Are Born can be a fun and useful exercise to engage in with colleagues, especially when you analyze major categories familiar to everyone. Be careful not to assume that players of all kinds—especially Icons—actually exist in every category. They don't. The universe of true, whole-brained brands is remarkably small. While there are many well-run businesses, few truly touch us to the point where we'd actively miss them if they disappeared.

As you sort through categories like cars, insurance companies, hotel chains, clothing retailers, and the like, ask yourselves *why* you are making the determinations you're making. In particular:

- Is it easier to identify the left-brain or right-brain factors at which a brand excels?

- Do some brands seem to try to fake a whole-brain approach by pasting right-brain marketing efforts on top of a lifeless Master brand? How effective is this? What makes it feel effective or ineffective?

- Is there agreement on which brands are Icons? Where do you agree or disagree?

Paving the way forward: Recapping the Six Principles

With luck, by now you have receptivity toward the idea of greater wholeness for your brand/company—or at the very least some greater curiosity about what might this look like.

So where do you start? Starting points are found in any or all of the Six Principles. On the following pages you'll find a recap you can share. To boost LB appeal, they're distilled for efficiency, with some suggestions on areas ripe for initial application.

A is for Art

OVERALL	Transcends the commercial realm and touches people in effective, nonlinear ways.
CONSISTS OF	Beauty, Craftsmanship, and The Arts
BEAUTY	Pleasing to the aesthetic senses. Evokes admiration for itself, not just for its uses. Goes beyond bare-bones efficiency and utility to engage with higher-order issues like sensory pleasure. **Brand Spotlight: Tea Forté**
CRAFTSMANSHIP	Quality of design/work; excellence in execution. Conveys a depth of care and pride in craft. Signals that we can trust you because you internalize high standards. **Brand Spotlight: Zildjian Cymbals**
THE ARTS	Purposely using one or more branches of creative activity like music, dance, painting. Conveys a willingness to take risks putting art first, brand second. Bypasses detectors of commercial intent and intrigues people in fresh ways, making emotional contact. **Brand Spotlight: method**

INITIAL APPLICATION: Product design & development. Advertising and marketing communications. Package design (Beauty & Craftsmanship). Promotion (The Arts).

B is for Balance

OVERALL   Offsets unconscious, pervasive practices
                    that have led to loud, disjointed, conformist
                    marketing.

CONSISTS OF   Harmony, Equanimity, and Zagging

HARMONY   A pleasing integration of elements. Creates a
                    satisfying whole through congruent marketing
                    shaped by a unified vision. Enables us to think
                    of your brand with pleasure and ease.
                    Brand Spotlight: Prêt à Manger

EQUANIMITY   Mental calmness and emotional equilibrium.
                    Offers a respite from brand hype and linearity,
                    imbuing brands with confidence and a more
                    sophisticated emotional appeal.
                    Brand Spotlight: Warby Parker

ZAGGING   Counterforce; a sharp change in direction.
                    Challenges the established parameters in a
                    category and offers a dramatically different
                    approach. Has the power to change markets.
                    Brand Spotlight: IKEA

AREAS OF INITIAL APPLICATION: Concept development. Customer
experience. Overall brand strategy. Advertising and marketing
communications.

C is for Connecting

OVERALL	Tunes in to inner sensations and perceptions that can help create breakthroughs.
CONSISTS OF	Synthesis, Association, and Intuition
SYNTHESIS	Forming a whole, sensing a pattern or larger picture. Identifies emerging ideas and patterns and often involves metaphoric thinking. Helps detect and give expression to fresh ideas and concepts characterized by wholeness and creative integrity. **Brand Spotlight: (Original) Banana Republic**
ASSOCIATION	Linking in idea; making connections. Connects seemingly unrelated ideas to form new possibilities. Helps create radically new and original approaches. **Brand Spotlight: Ben & Jerry's**
INTUITION	Inner knowing or insight, often sudden. Offers non-rational intelligence that may arrive as a flash of insight or a gentle inner voice. Can be a potent source of ideas unavailable through other means. **Brand Spotlight: Steve Jobs/Apple**

AREAS OF INITIAL APPLICATION: Everything, including: Ideation, concept development, product development, customer experience, advertising and marketing communications.

D is for Depth

OVERALL	Goes beyond the superficiality of the traditional business realm to touch larger aspects of humanity that connect us.
CONSISTS OF	Essence, Multidimensionality, and Roots
ESSENCE	Core purpose or mission. Reflects a sense of service to larger values. Connects with fundamental human needs and yearnings. Helps create loyalty among both customers and employees. **Brand Spotlight: Costco**
MULTI-DIMENSIONALITY	A holistic, nuanced view of people. Rejects lifeless, reductionist approaches and embraces complexity, layers and contradictions. Helps make brands more intriguing, distinctive, and resilient. **Brand Spotlight: Trader Joe's**
ROOTS	Connects with sources of vitality through story-telling. Links us to larger worlds of time, place and meaning. Helps shape brand image, guide direction, and establish and sustain resonance. **Brand Spotlight: Moleskine**

AREAS OF INITIAL APPLICATION: Overall brand/company strategy. Audience targeting, advertising, marketing communications (Multidimensionality & Roots). Cause marketing (Roots).

E is for Emotion

OVERALL	Intentionally addresses the brand or company's emotional relationship with customers.
CONSISTS OF	Attunement, Empathy, and Engagement
ATTUNEMENT	Being receptive and aware. Listens for and attends to the emotional impact you have on customers. Can help create distinction and avoid potentially disastrous blind spots. **Brand Spotlight: TD Bank**
EMPATHY	Understanding the feelings of others. Grasps the emotional reality of your customers and addresses it. May be the single most important source of innovation, creating a bond competitors can't match. **Brand Spotlight: Bridgeport Financial**
ENGAGEMENT	Forming a meaningful connection. Connects directly with consumers on an emotional basis through authentic person-to-person interactions. Offers benefits ranging from early problem detection to creating raving fans. **Brand Spotlight: Zappos**

AREAS OF INITIAL APPLICATION: Customer experience. Concept development, product/service design and improvement (Empathy).

F is for Fun

OVERALL	Offers lightness that allows us to connect with customers and employees in more fully human ways.
CONSISTS OF	Joviality, Enjoyment, and Play
JOVIALITY	Cheerfulness and good humor. Provides a welcome antidote to the impersonality of most business. Warmth, levity, and ease create space for a sense of shared humanity. **Brand Spotlight: Southwest Airlines**
ENJOYMENT	Creating pleasurable experiences. Envisions a congenial context for the product/service and works to deliver it. Makes us happy, repeat customers eager to spread the word. **Brand Spotlight: Bespoke Innovations**
PLAY	Freedom or scope for action; enjoyable activity. Affords opportunities for autonomy and self-direction that can make work feel like play. Fuels innovation while also helping attract and retain talented, motivated employees. **Brand Spotlight: 3M**

AREAS FOR INITIAL APPLICATION: Overall brand/company strategy. Customer experience. Human resources (Play).

The journey ahead

When we fully use the right and left brain on a brand, in a company, wonderful things can happen. We brighten more lives, and our customers become more energized and loyal. Having come this far, you are well equipped to begin the next phase: unleashing your right-brain genius and using it to transform your brand, your business, and your future.

And the time is ripe: new possibilities for connection and relationship with your customers through social media and e-commerce make it more important than ever to bring richness, vitality, and imagination to everything you do.

As a first (and free) next step, please sign up for my newsletter by going to www.rightbrainbrands.com, which will give you instant access to several free resources for the book. You'll also receive, on a mostly-monthly basis, compelling brand stories, provocations, and exercises to work your right-brain muscles. And, although it goes without saying, your e-mail address will never be shared with anyone else or sold.

If you'd like to know more about working with me to unleash your right-brain genius and bring these principles to life in your business or brand, you'll find additional information at the end of the book. Also, you can learn more by visiting www. rightbrainbrands.com.

Meanwhile, It has been my privilege to guide you thus far. I wish you well on the journey ahead. I am eager to hear your feedback and learn of your efforts and successes.

"The voyage of discovery is not in seeking new landscapes but in having new eyes."

–MARCEL PROUST

WHAT GREAT BRANDS KNOW

APPENDIX:
READY FOR MORE?

I hope you've enjoyed this book. If you'd like to go further with the ideas presented here, I've assembled a curated list of resources in the pages that follow. This list starts with specific book and video recommendations tailored to each of the six principles. In addition, you'll find a complete list of books referenced in *What Great Brands Know*, along with a couple of newsletters and other books you might enjoy.

One quick, easy and free next step: please sign up for my newsletter by going to www.rightbrainbrands.com. You'll get instant access to some helpful (and fun) resources for the book. You'll also be the first to receive updates and future bonus content. And if you'd like some help bringing the principles in this book to life in your brand/business, you'll find more information on my website as well.

As you explore the resources in this section and begin to unleash your right-brain genius, you may well come across (or already know of) additional books, articles, newsletters, videos and other materials that would be of interest to other readers. Please get in touch (Tracy@rightbrainbrands.com). I welcome your feedback—and your discoveries!

FOR FURTHER READING

Here are a few books that will allow you to explore specific topics in greater depth.

A is for Art

Pink, Daniel H., *A Whole New Mind: Why Right-Brainers Will Rule the Future*. New York: Riverhead Books, 2006. This book touches on right-brain thinking in many forms, but some of its most memorable and potent arguments address the role of Art.

B is for Balance

Cain, Susan, <u>Quiet</u>: *The Power of Introverts in a World That Can't Stop Talking*. New York: Crown Publishers, 2012. You may not need to read the entire book, but spending some time with it (and/or Cain's TED talk, noted below) will awaken you to prevailing cultural assumptions that are both hidden and needlessly limiting.

C is for Connecting

Ziegler, Mel and Patricia, *Wild Company: The Untold Story of Banana Republic*. New York: Simon & Schuster, 2012. What happens when right-brain genius meets a buzz-saw of left-brain rigidity? This should be required reading in business school.

D is for Depth

Mark, Margaret and Carol S. Pearson, *The Hero and the Outlaw: Building Extraordinary Brands Through the Power of Archetypes*. New York: McGraw-Hill, 2001. A bit dated, but an excellent introduction to an important and powerful topic.

E is for Emotion

Patnaik, Dev, *Wired to Care: How Companies Prosper When They Create Widespread Empathy*. Upper Saddle River, N.J.: FT Press, 2009. This book is filled with compelling stories of companies that have succeeded by looking at the world through their customers' eyes—and those who've stumbled because they haven't.

F is for Fun

Hsieh, Tony, *Delivering Happiness: A Path to Profits, Passion and Purpose*. New York: Business Plus, 2010. Zappos' CEO shares his journey to creating a company whose extraordinary success rests on a culture actively centered on happiness.

VIDEOS

TED talks are a wonderful free resource. The following talks are suggested to provoke thought and conversation around ideas presented in the book. Some deal directly with topics in the book, while others are more suggestive and may embody one or more of the ideas discussed. The list is just to get you started and is far from exhaustive. You'll enjoy poking around the site (www.ted.com) if you don't already know it.

Overall

Iain McGilchrist: The divided brain

http://www.ted.com/talks/iain_mcgilchrist_the_divided_brain.html

Mae Jamison: Teach the Arts and Sciences Together

http://www.ted.com/talks/mae_jemison_on_teaching_arts_and_sciences_together.html

Chip Conley: Measuring what makes life worthwhile

http://www.ted.com/talks/chip_conley_measuring_what_makes_lifeworthwhile.html

A is for Art

John Bohannon: Dance vs. powerpoint, a modest proposal

http://www.ted.com/talks/john_bohannon_dance_vs_powerpoint_a_modest_proposal.html

Denis Dutton: A Darwinian theory of beauty

http://www.ted.com/talks/denis_dutton_a_darwinian_theory_of_beauty.html

Richard Seymour: How beauty feels

http://www.ted.com/talks/richard_seymour_how_beauty_feels.html

B is for Balance

Susan Cain: The power of introverts

http://www.ted.com/talks/susan_cain_the_power_of_introverts.html

Carl Honoré: In praise of slowness

http://www.ted.com/talks/carl_honore_praises_slowness.html

Don Norman: 3 ways good design makes you happy

http://www.ted.com/talks/don_norman_on_design_and_emotion.html

C is for Connecting

Dan Cobley: What physics taught me about marketing
http://www.ted.com/talks/dan_cobley_what_physics_taught_me_about_marketing.html

Elizabeth Gilbert: Your elusive creative genius
http://www.ted.com/talks/elizabeth_gilbert_on_genius.html

Margaret Heffernan: Dare to disagree
http://www.ted.com/talks/margaret_heffernan_dare_to_disagree.html

D is for Depth
Sir Ken Robinson: Bring on the learning revolution!
http://www.ted.com/talks/sir_ken_robinson_bring_on_the_revolution.html

Adam Savage: My obsession with objects and the stories they tell
http://www.ted.com/talks/adam_savage_s_obsessions.html

Simon Sinek: How great leaders inspire action
http://www.ted.com/talks/simon_sinek_how_great_leaders_inspire_action.html

E is for Emotion
Daniel Goleman: Why aren't we more compassionate?
http://www.ted.com/talks/daniel_goleman_on_compassion.html

Krista Tippett: Reconnecting with compassion
http://www.ted.com/talks/krista_tippett_reconnecting_with_compassion.
html

Julian Treasure: 5 Ways to listen better
http://www.ted.com/talks/julian_treasure_5_ways_to_listen_better.html

F is for Fun
Stuart Brown: Play is more than just fun
http://www.ted.com/talks/stuart_brown_says_play_is_more_than_fun_it_s_
vital.html

Tim Brown: Tales of creativity and play
http://www.ted.com/talks/tim_brown_on_creativity_and_play.html

Tim Leberecht: 3 ways to (usefully) lose control of your brand
http://www.ted.com/talks/tim_leberecht_3_ways_to_usefully_lose_control_
of_your_reputation.html

NEWSLETTERS

We could all easily spend 40 hours/week reading freebie online subscriptions. You surely have your favorites already and don't need a long list of other temptations. So here are just two; both are weeklies I always find worthwhile.

Co.Design Weekly: *Fast Company* offers several free newsletters. Their Co.Design newsletter has been a keeper, and weekly frequency ("Best of") is manageable. Take a look at the options here: http://www.fastcompany.com/newsletters

Marketoonist: If you don't already subscribe to Tom Fishburne's weekly marketing cartoon and blog, you should. His cartoons are delightful, and his posts are among the best in marketing today. Find it here: http://tomfishburne.com

BOOKS REFERENCED

The following books are referenced in *What Great Brands Know*:

Amabile, Teresa, and Steven Kramer, *The Progress Principle: Using Small Wins to Ignite Joy, Engagement, and Creativity at Work*. Boston: Harvard Business Review Press, 2011.

Bhargava, Rohit, Likeonomics: *The Unexpected Truth behind Earning Trust, Influencing Behavior, and Inspiring Action*. Hoboken, N.J.: John Wiley & Sons, 2012.

Brown, Tim with Barry Katz, *Change by Design: How Design Thinking Transforms Organizations and Inspires Innovation*. New York: Harper Business, 2009.

Cain, Susan, *Quiet: The Power of Introverts in a World That Can't Stop Talking.* New York: Crown Publishers, 2012.

Christensen, Clayton M., *The Innovator's Dilemma: When New Technologies Cause Great Firms to Fail.* Boston: Harvard Business School Press, 1997.

Collins, Jim, and Jerry I. Porras, *Built to Last: Successful Habits of Visionary Companies.* New York: Harper Business, 2004.

Hogshead, Sally, *Fascinate: Your 7 Triggers to Persuasion and Captivation.* New York: Harper Business, 2010.

Hsieh, Tony, *Delivering Happiness: A Path to Profits, Passion and Purpose.* New York: Business Plus, 2010.

Isaacson, Walter, *Steve Jobs.* New York: Simon & Schuster, 2011.

Margolis, Michael, *Believe Me: Why Your Vision, Brand and Leadership Need a Bigger Story.* New York: Get Storied Press, 2009.

Mark, Margaret and Carol S. Pearson, *The Hero and the Outlaw: Building Extraordinary Brands Through the Power of Archetypes.* New York: McGraw-Hill, 2001.

McCracken, Grant, *Chief Culture Officer: How to Create a Living, Breathing Corporation.* New York: Basic Books, 2009.

McGilchrist, Iain, *The Divided Brain and the Search for Meaning.* Yale University Press [Kindle Edition], 2012.

McGilchrist, Iain, *The Master and His Emissary: The Divided Brain and the Making of the Western World.* New Haven, CT: Yale University Press, 2009.

Moon, Youngme, *Different: Escaping the Competitive Herd.* New York: Crown Business, 2010.

Patnaik, Dev, *Wired to Care: How Companies Prosper When They Create Widespread Empathy.* Upper Saddle River, N.J.: FT Press, 2009.

Pink, Daniel H., *A Whole New Mind: Why Right-Brainers Will Rule the Future.* New York: Riverhead Books, 2006.

Sinek, Simon, *Start with Why: How Great Leaders Inspire Everyone to Take Action.* New York: Portfolio, 2009.

Ziegler, Mel and Patricia, *Wild Company: The Untold Story of Banana Republic.* New York: Simon & Schuster, 2012.

Additional books you may enjoy

Powers, William, *Hamlet's BlackBerry: Building a Good Life in the Digital Age.* New York: Harper's Perennial, 2011. This book explores the mixed blessings and underappreciated perils of our current maximally connected digital age. Powers makes a convincing case that our present era of overload is not new. He offers a fascinating look at earlier eras of information explosion by examining seven thinkers, from Plato to McLuhan. You'll never view your digital life quite the same way again.

Whyte, David, *The Heart Aroused: Poetry and the Preservation of Soul in Corporate America.* New York: Crown Business, 1996.

This British poet is also a consultant to high-powered companies. He sees timeless human fears and yearnings as appropriate subjects for businesses to address, and draws on poetry to make his case. His perspective and style will not appeal to left-brain enthusiasts of corporate efficiency, but his penetrating questions and rich stories are sure to resonate with those trapped in soul-withering environments.

And nearly anything by

Seth Godin

By now you've probably read something by the relentlessly passionate and prolific marketer-turned-guru. If you haven't, I recommend three of his most recent books, *Linchpin: Are You Indispensible?*, *Tribes: We Need You to Lead Us*, and *The Icarus Deception: How High Will You Fly?* Easy to read, hard to dismiss.

Thomas Moore

Moore, a former monk, musician, and therapist, presents an entirely new way to look at the world and oneself that won't resonate with everyone. *Care of the Soul: A Guide to Cultivating Depth and Sacredness in Everyday Life* examines the importance of imagination and beauty, mythology and ritual in everyday life. *The Re-Enchantment of Everyday Life* explores how to invite magic back into our lives. If you prefer breezy, practical books, Moore's will make you squirm. But others, who may not even know how parched you are for depth and meaning in a culture obsessed with the rational and superficial, may find that his books offer a deep draught of water in a desert you've only just perceived.

NOTES

How Great Brands Are Born

1. McGilchrist, Iain, *The Master and His Emissary: The Divided Brain and the Making of the Western World.* New Haven, CT: Yale University Press, 2009. Most writing about the left and right brains focuses on the type of information processing that takes place in each. One of the key contributions of McGilchrist's remarkable work is differentiating the type of attention that the two hemispheres give to the world and the consequences of this difference.

A is for Art

1. Hewitt, Peter. "Silken Tea Infuser." *Tea Forté*, Accessed 2012-2013, http://www.teaforte.com/about/behind-the-designs/.

2. Ibid.

3. Patnaik, Dev. *Wired To Care: How Companies Prosper When They Create Widespread Empathy.* Upper Saddle River, N.J.: FT Press, 2009, 51.

4. "Zildjian Family." *Zildjian Cymbals.* Accessed 2012-2013, http://zildjian.com/About/Family-Bios/Armand-Zildjian

5. Tom Fishburne: "Free Sample," *Marketoonist* (blog), January 22nd, 2012, http://tomfishburne.com/2012/01/free-sample.html

B is for Balance

1. Clifford, Stephanie. "Would You Like a Smile With That?" *New York Times.* Aug. 6, 2011, http://www.nytimes.com/2011/08/07/business/pret-a-manger-with-new-fast-food-ideas-gains-a-foothold-in-united-states.html?pagewanted=all&_r=0

2. Cain, Susan. "Susan Cain: The power of introverts." Filmed February 2012. TED video, 19:04. Posted March 2012, http://www.ted.com/talks/susan_cain_the_power_of_introverts.html

C is for Connecting

1. Ziegler, Mel, and Patricia Ziegler. *Wild Company: The Untold Story of Banana Republic.* New York: Simon & Schuster, 2012, 5-8.

2. Ibid, 9.

3. Ibid, 26.

4. Ibid, 148

5. Ibid, 177.

6. Ibid, 111.

7. Isaacson, Walter. *Steve Jobs*. New York: Simon & Schuster, 2011, 35.

8. Ibid, 48.

9. Ibid, 350.

10. Ibid, 397.

11. Ibid, 464.

D is for Depth

1. Greenhouse, Steven. "How Costco Became the Anti-Wal-Mart," *New York Times*, July 17, 2005, http://www.nytimes.com/2005/07/17/business/yourmoney/17costco.html?pagewanted=all&_r=0

2. Shapiro, Nina. "Company for the People," *Seattle Weekly*, Oct. 9, 2006, http://www.seattleweekly.com/2004-12-15/news/company-for-the-people/

3. Ibid.

4. Greenhouse.

5. Kowitt, Beth. "Inside the Secret World of Trader Joe's – Full Version," *money.cnn.com*. Last modified August 23, 2010, http://money.cnn.com/2010/08/20/news/companies/inside_trader_joes_full_version.fortune/index.htm

6. Paris, Ellen. "Brie, but Not Budweiser," *Forbes*, October 2, 1989, p. 235, cited in International Directory of Company Histories, "Trader Joe's Company History."Chicago: St. James Press, 2003, Volume 50.

7. Mark, Margaret and Carol S. Pearson, *The Hero and the Outlaw: Building Extraordinary Brands Through the Power of Archetypes*. New York: McGraw-Hill, 2001.

E is for Emotion

1. Reichheld, Fred. "In a World of 'No,' Just Say 'Yes'," LinkedIn.com. Last modified November 15, 2012, http://www.linkedin.com/today/post/article/20121115153538-7928939-in-a-world-of-no-just-say-yes

2. Denning, Steve. "Can Banks Delight Customers?" Forbes.com. Last modified October 26, 2011, http://www.forbes.com/sites/stevedenning/2011/10/26/can-banks-delight-customers/

3. "Customer Loyalty in Retail Banking: Global Edition," Bain Report, December 4, 2012, http://www.bain.com/publications/articles/customer-loyalty-in-retail-banking-2012.aspx

4. Sinek, Simon. *Start With Why: How Great Leaders Inspire Everyone to Take Action.* New York, Portfolio, 2009, 189.

5. Ibid, 190.

6. Ibid.

7. Ibid, 191.

8. Smith Hendrickson, Susan, "Collections firm finds human touch pays off," *San Francisco Business Times*, October 5, 2003, http://www.bizjournals.com/sanfrancisco/stories/2003/10/06/focus3.html?page=all

9. Berenbaum, Diane. "Four Key Strategies for Building Emotional Connection with Your Customers," *CommunicoLtd.com* Accessed 2012-2013, http://www.communicoltd.com/pages/1076_four_key_strategies_for_building_emotional_connections_with_your_customers.cfm

10. Chafkin, Max. "The Zappos Way of Managing," *Inc.com*. Last modified May 1, 2009, http://www.inc.com/magazine/20090501/the-zappos-way-of-managing.html

11. Verrill, Ashly. "A Zappos Lesson in Customer Service Metrics," *Customer Service Investigator*. Last modified November 2, 2012, http://csi.softwareadvice.com/a-zappos-lesson-in-customer-service-metrics-1101029/

12. Niemi, Wayne. "Zappos Milestone: Q&A with Tony Hsieh," *Zappos.com*. Last modified May 4, 2009, http://about.zappos.com/press-center/media-coverage/zappos-milestone-qa-tony-hsieh

13. Patnaik, Dev. Wired To Care: How Companies Prosper When They Create Widespread Empathy. Upper Saddle River, N.J.: FT Press, 2009.

F is for Fun

1. McKee, Steve. "Flying Southwest on American," *Innovationexcellence.com*. Last modified July 8, 2011, http://www.innovationexcellence.com/blog/2011/07/08/flying-southwest-on-american/

2. "Southwest Airlines 'Malice in Dallas' (Six Parts)." YouTube videos. Posted by "SouthwestAirlinesArchives," February 19, 2009, http://www.youtube.com/user/southwestairchive?feature=watch

3. "Southwest 'Gets It' with Our Culture," Nuts About Southwest, March 4, 2011, http://www.blogsouthwest.com/southwest-airlines-"gets-it"-our-culture/

4. "Case Studies," *Bespoke Innovations*. Accessed 2012-2013, http://www.bespokeinnovations.com/content/deborah

5. "Case Studies," *Bespoke Innovations*. Accessed 2012-2013, http://www.bespokeinnovations.com/content/chad

6. Collins, Jim, and Jerry I. Porras. *Built to Last: Successful Habits Of Visionary Companies*. New York: Harper Business, 2004.

7. Goetz, Kaomi. "How 3M Gave Everyone Days Off and Created an Innovation Dynamo," *FastCoDesign.com*. Last modified February 1, 2011, http://www.fastcodesign.com/1663137/how-3m-gave-everyone-days-off-and-created-an-innovation-dynamo

8. Amabile, Teresa, and Steven Kramer, *The Progress Principle: Using Small Wins to Ignite Joy, Engagement, and Creativity at Work*. Boston: Harvard Business Review Press, 2011.

The Way Forward

1. The three issues featured here come from the work of Iain McGilchrist, whose remarkable book *The Master and His Emissary* I have cited earlier. For those who may wish to sample something shorter, I highly recommend his 31-page e-book *The Divided Brain and the Search for Meaning*. Full bibliographic details in Notes.

ACKNOWLEDGMENTS

As with Oscar acceptance speeches, there are too many people to thank, but that won't stop me from trying. So many wonderful folk have helped me that this is necessarily a partial list.

This book would not exist without Dan Pink and his book, *A Whole New Mind*. I read it when it first came out on a family beach vacation in Mexico. Among other things, it gave me a terrible sunburn: the sun moved and I did not, riveted to the book. It also gave me language and a framework for things I'd perceived without knowing quite what they were. And it gave me an understanding of my own identity, as a mostly right-brained person with a left-brain pedigree (Wharton MBA) inhabiting the mostly left-brain world of business. Thank you, Dan! Though we have never met, you sparked an epiphany and a quest to give the right brain a voice in this world.

I am also deeply indebted to Iain McGilchrist, whose remarkable works, *The Master and His Emissary: The Divided Brain and the Making of the Western World* and *The Divided Brain and the Search for Meaning*, both deepened my understanding of left- and right-brain issues immeasurably and added to the urgency of my quest.

Since I started Right-Brain Brands I have been blessed and buoyed by the response from readers. If you've ever commented on my newsletter or blog (electronically or in person), I treasure what you've shared. Your response and encouragement mean far more than you know.

Several people have contributed directly to the content of the book. Laura Pinsky and Lynne Michalek, former colleagues whom I'm also privileged to call friends, shared their helpful perspective on the challenges and mindset of corporate marketers today. Over many a bagel and coffee my largely left-brained buddies Jay Mixter, Tom Ward, and Ray LaFrance helped strengthen my ideas on why right-brain marketing matters. I'm especially indebted to Jay for suggesting a 2 x 2 matrix to explain the interplay of right- and left-brain thinking in brands.

I also greatly appreciate comments on the last part of the book by my friends Len Johnson and Don Lowy. Thank you! Your good suggestions resulted in two dozen pages of new material.

Every author should have Elizabeth Marshall by his/her side. In fact, she should consider cloning. As book coach, high-level editor, reality check, cheerleader, networking doyenne, marketing maven and expert guide to the brave new worlds of publishing and social media, she has helped make this a better book than it ever would have been. She's also been an inspiring and empowering presence as I launch not just a book but an exciting new chapter in my professional life as well.

Book specialist Janica Smith (of Adminismith) has been invaluable in helping me navigate the details of production, blending a remarkable big-picture view with in-depth knowledge of (and patience for) the nitty-gritty. Working with her has been a delight. She was also instrumental in connecting me with other experts who deserve mention and thanks: Lauren Hidden (of

Hidden Helpers) for copy editing, and Bella Guzmán for her excellent work on interior design and her wonderful collaborative style. Any errors or infelicities are completely my responsibility.

Through Janica I've also discovered realms I never knew, including the world of copyright and permissions. In this regard, I want to thank copyright and trademark attorney Lucy Lovrien for her generous informal advice and Julie Brown of The Permissions Group. I also offer sincere thanks to the people who granted permission to quote from their works, including cartoonist and blogger Tom Fishburne (Marketoonist), author and columnist Steve McKee, Tim Reason of Bain & Company, Jane Whitman of Tea Forté, and Laura Rivera of Zildjian.

Warm thanks are also due to Mira Leon, who made important contributions in many areas as my summer marketing assistant.

Few hardy souls would ever volunteer to provide a close reading of any author's manuscript, for good reason: it can be a thankless slog. That's why I'm enormously grateful to Karen Krinsky Leon for her excellent observations, candor, and eagle eye, all served up with her trademark wit.

Annie Smidt, founder of Durable Creative, has been design muse and code honcho for my website from the start. Lucky me that her creative skills now extend to cover design as well! Brava!

Peter Elwell, my illustrator, is the most omni-creative person I've been privileged to know. For this project I tapped his great skills in editorial art, but his talents abound in more artistic realms than can readily be counted. This was not an easy project for any illustrator, but Peter rose to all challenges with skill, grace, and wit, making the experience delightful along the way. I already look forward to our next collaboration.

Writing can be a lonely endeavor, and meeting regularly with friendly faces has been a godsend. Regulars of the Yale women's writing group in Boston cheered me on throughout the process: Cindy Barr, Jane Bybee, Kee Chan, Mary Chitty, Susan Emanuel, and Lisa Goldman. May your own writing projects blossom and flourish. I'm also grateful to the Yale Entrepreneurs' group in Boston for their support, especially leader Ryck Lent and Christine Kuta.

To the endorsers whose names and words grace my book: I am honored and humbled by your generous, kind and thoughtful remarks. To know that my work resonates with such talented and accomplished people has been an immeasurable gift on its own. Whatever success this book may come to enjoy will surely trace in large measure to what you've written. For all of this, my boundless thanks.

My deepest gratitude goes to Alex Kozlov, my husband, whose unflagging support is the stuff of heroes. For my book and business alone you've been priceless as sounding board, strategic advisor, rock, best editor on the planet, sustainer in chief and far more. Then there's the rest of my life, which simply wouldn't be complete without you—or nearly as much fun.

Unite the hemispheres! Spread the word!

We all benefit when there is greater room for warmth, friendliness, and art in business. When we can dial down the frenzied hype, superficiality, and me-tooism that leads to indifference and tuning out. When we can engage with our customers in deeper, more powerful, and lasting ways. That's why I wrote this book, and I hope you found it valuable.

I would be honored if you would share the message with others. Here are some ways to help spread the word:

- Sign up for my newsletter: You'll be able to forward issues to friends and colleagues who might be interested. And who knows? There may be an article that can spark exactly the kind of conversation you should be having in your company. Just go to www.rightbrainbrands.com

- E-mail four of your colleagues or friends about the book.

- Mention this book in your blog or newsletter, if you have one, and include this link: www.rightbrainbrands.com/what-great-brands-know. Feel free to get in touch if you'd like to interview me.

- Share *What Great Brands Know* on social media (Facebook, Twitter, LinkedIn) with a link to the book page: www.rightbrainbrands.com/what-great-brands-know

Please e-mail me at Tracy@rightbrainbrands.com to share your feedback, insights, examples from your own experience, and whatever else you are moved to share. I'm so looking forward to hearing from you!

Need some help?

If you would like some help using these principles to transform your brand, business, or organization, I'd love to help you. Here are some possibilities:

SPEAKING AND WORKSHOPS: To create excitement and/or strengthen institutional buy-in around right-brain approaches, consider a spirited and stimulating presentation to enliven your event, or a workshop to bring these principles to life for your team. Learn more here: www.rightbrainbrands.com/speaking

COACHING: I'm happy to do a big project for your company, but I'm also happy to make you a hero in your organization. Receive custom 1:1 guidance around the changes you're trying to bring to the world. Learn more at: www.rightbrainbrands.com/hire-tracy

CONSULTING: Looking to apply these principles to your brand directly? Let's discuss your goals and challenges and the ways I can help your brand create a brighter future. Learn more here: www.righbrainbrands.com/hire-tracy

Still a bit skeptical? Consider a Right-Brain Rental session. I guarantee you'll find value from hearing a right-brain perspective on your situation or you get a full refund. Read more here: www.rightbrainbrands.com/hire-tracy About the Author

About the author

Tracy Carlson is Founder & Principal of Right-Brain Brands. She is a seasoned marketing strategist, speaker and advisor who helps companies develop brands that people care about and that inspire loyalty. Tracy has led some of America's best-known brands (Dove, Hellmann's, Wisk) and consulted to many more (including General Mills, Rubbermaid, and Pepsi), and has extensive experience advising startups and small businesses as well.

Tracy's non-traditional background combines equal parts Wharton MBA and unrepentant Yale humanities geek. This hybrid expertise, integrating human-centered right-brain thinking with left-brain analysis and metrics, forms the basis for her new book *What Great Brands Know: Unleash Your Right-Brain Genius to Stand Out and Make Customers Care*.

She has also written for *The Washington Post*, and marketing publications including *Ad Age*, *BrandWeek*, and *AdMap*. Tracy lives with her husband in the Boston area.

About the Illustrator

Peter Elwell is a New York-based illustrator whose work has appeared in several publications, including *The New York Times Book Review*, *The National Lampoon*, *New York Magazine*,

Money Magazine, and *Working Woman* Magazine. Beginning with writing and illustrating *The King Of The Pipers*, Elwell has illustrated numerous books, including *Three Brave Women*, the NY Times bestseller *My Mother Is Mine*, *The Amazing Adventures Of Bathman*, and *Adios Oscar*, which he also wrote.

When not drawing, Peter Elwell writes and is presently working on the novel, *Teenage Dance Beat*.

www.ingramcontent.com/pod-product-compliance
Lightning Source LLC
Chambersburg PA
CBHW030934220326

41521CB00040B/2310